Journey into Belief

FINDING GOD THROUGH THE CREED

Steve McCoy-Thompson

Liguori
ONE LIGUORI DRIVE
LIGUORI MO 63057-9999

DEDICATION

To Meri for all things,
And to my children, Matthias and Marie,
For their joy and inspiration.

Imprimi Potest:
Richard Thibodeau, C.Ss.R.
Provincial, Denver Province
The Redemptorists

ISBN 0-7648-1158-4
Library of Congress Catalog Number: 2004107429

© 2004, Steve McCoy-Thompson
Printed in the United States of America
04 05 06 07 08 5 4 3 2 1

Scripture quotations are from the *New Revised Standard Version of the Bible*, © 1989 by the Division of Christian Education of the National Council of the Churches of Christ in the USA. Used by permission. All rights reserved.

To order, call 1-800-325-9521
www.liguori.org

Acknowledgment

The writing of this book has been a journey and many people have helped along the way. I would like to thank the high-quality priests and parish staff of the Catholic Community of Pleasanton (CCOP) for being such gracious hosts and guides for the Catholic Community, particularly our pastor, Fr. Dan Danielson and Stephen Puricelli, who kept me out of trouble with his edits. I am forever grateful to Karen Miller, who was director of RCIA at the time and who gave so much of her energy, spirit, and song. Special thanks also to the other candidates, members of the RCIA Team, and our faith sponsors who were so integral to this program, and who have been given pseudonyms to protect the innocent—except one, Doug Boccignone, who was my sponsor and mentor throughout. Also, I would like to thank the Catholic Church in general for resurrecting the RCIA program, for taking it seriously, and for forcing people like me to take my faith seriously as well.

Equal amounts of gratitude go to those who have encouraged both my faith and this book in an ongoing mystagogy. A family faith group called Holy Chaos and a men's breakfast group called Boys of Breakfast, both of which meet twice a month, have provided lasting friendship and spiritual support. As for the book itself, sincere thanks go to Kathleen Chesto for her valuable encouragement, to V. Venkata Subbarao for inspiring the title, to Elsie McGrath for being such a supportive editor, and to the entire staff of Liguori Publications for nurturing this piece along the way. Finally, let me thank my wife and children for their deep love and faith, as well as my extended family, especially my parents and siblings, who were wonderfully understanding throughout this amazing journey.

Contents

Introduction

Wedding Invitations

Is the Creator a personal, loving God? Is Jesus the Son of Man, not to mention the Son of God? And for the past four months, a small group of inquiring minds have delicately approached such questions through a church-sponsored Q&A session called Inquiry. It's for people who want to know more about Catholic teaching, or for people like me, who are considering the Big Leap, as in "faith."

Faith, according to the songwriter Paul Simon, is similar to a distant island seen against a setting sun. Conversion is the act of getting there. The journey comes with no navigation chart and, for me, is filled with obstacles. This call to everlasting commitment is truly daunting. It is also exciting and terrifying. In other words, it's a bit like getting married.

In Catholic tradition, Jesus Christ is considered the bridegroom to the Church, who is the bride. This is a beautiful image that speaks to the care and love we hope to find in the family. But it also speaks to other souls who have come, however tentatively, to this altar called faith and must now consider a lifetime relationship with the Church family.

In my case, the "wedding" is to be a very public ceremony

at the parish church on Easter weekend. During the ceremony, a small group of converts will be dunked in water or simply anointed with oil, depending on their circumstances, before a thousand onlookers. The problem is that I still don't know the bride very well. She has some habits I don't understand. She believes things—and insists I believe them too—that I'm decidedly unsure about. My wife loves her, despite her faults, but my side of the family most assuredly does not. In short, it's a typical engagement, full of doubts and divisions.

Still, there are aspects of this marriage that are wonderfully captivating. I am struck by the community, the caring, and the commitment to something that will certainly change my life. In the quiet recesses of my soul, I have longed for these things. It's as if a tiny seed had been planted long before I was born, and is striving to take root.

The first step toward this Big Leap is deciding whether to join a program called the Rite of Christian Initiation of Adults—RCIA. If Inquiry has been an easy path, then RCIA is a slippery slope of soul-searching for those deeper answers that have evaded me for years. Or perhaps I have evaded them. At the end of this slope, I will make the final decision: whether to become a member of the worldwide community of the Catholic Church.

And so, with the period of Inquiry drawing to a close, the first step is now. The wedding invitations are waiting to be sent. The church and the priest have been reserved months in advance for the occasion. The bride is ready. Am I?

CHAPTER 1

Faith-Based Insanity and the Spiritual Fence

I imagine Joseph lying in bed and wondering how he can reasonably get out of his mess. His fiancée is pregnant, but not by him. He's sure of that, but he's not sure who else knows. Probably everyone. Then an angel comes in a dream and says, "Fear not."

And, miracle of miracles, Joseph does not fear. Instead, he follows. Joseph doesn't know where he is going. He doesn't know how he and his fiancée will manage to raise a newborn in a strange land. But he has faith.

Another favorite character is John the Baptist. John gives up everything, leaves his family, and goes into the desert to eat locusts and live in the dirt. He's not even sure why he's going; he simply knows someone is coming—perhaps not soon, or even in his lifetime. But he goes anyway because he has faith.

These are the stories in the Bible that amaze me, particularly those moments when a person must make a difficult choice. Invariably, these are average people who have to make life-changing decisions without having answers, and always under trying circumstances. From Abraham to Moses, and beyond, the Bible is littered with people who follow God's word without knowing where they are going. Are they insane? Maybe. Yet it is precisely this bit of faith-based insanity that I admire.

Zen and the Spiritual Fence

For much of my adult life, I have sat rather comfortably on a spiritual fence. I grew up in a household that was resolutely non-religious. With an ex-Catholic mother and an ex-Baptist father, we studied the history, if not the spirit, of the Bible. Through them, I learned the difference between transfiguration and transubstantiation, and a long list of more verifiable facts. Religion was considered a crutch for the huddled masses—in other words, for anyone who believed in God and therefore must be huddling out of fear, or ignorance, or some deficiency we did not share.

In my teen years, my friends and I became interested in Zen Buddhism and the Force and other safe Higher Powers, which were ill-defined and impersonal and could be explained with little more than a shrug of one's shoulders. We believed in something, I suppose, but didn't know what—and that seemed to be just fine with us.

In retrospect, this was mighty ironic and since we questioned everything—our parents, school, government, and any system of authority we stumbled across. But when it came to questions of the soul, we were silent—perhaps because we thought we'd never die.

Imperfect Rationale

Then I married a Catholic, which raised irony to a higher place. Yet there was clearly something about Meri. Beyond her good looks and obvious charm, she possessed a centeredness that, in all my fitful questioning, I could never reach. She was joyful and she was solid. She did not huddle.

Still, I kept a distance from her faith. I retained a perfect rationale for remaining on my spiritual fence. My fear was that if I ever did get down from that fence, I might get down on the wrong side.

My perfect rationale stemmed from a belief that there are many paths to God. Who's to say one path is better than another? Certainly not me—someone who's idea of God was limited to the Jedi code. So I attended church and sat in the rear and listened. But after years of looking in from the spiritual outside, I felt a kind of uncertain emptiness on the inside.

Raising Angels

Then we had children. When they entered the world, I literally and physically felt God in the delivery room. Our son and daughter were angels made manifest. They could be hellions too: uplifting and exhausting, joyous and fall-on-the-floor hair-pulled-from-the-scalp maddening. Eventually, I came to appreciate something my wife had said about a year after the arrival of our firstborn.

Matthias was often sick in that first year. He went from the ninetieth percentile in weight down to the second percentile in eight months. He would cry long hours into the night and not eat much during the day. But whenever we had company over, or when we took him to the doctors, he was joyous. In short, he drove us crazy. And we still loved him madly. At one point, Meri said, "This must be how God feels about us."

In God's eyes, we are children who screw up—a lot. And we're forgiven—always. We refuse to do things that are obviously good for us, like eating and sleeping, and we're still loved. We do dreadful things, like drive our parents crazy and start wars, and we may still be forgiven. And it dawned on me, finally, that maybe this wellspring of love is the foundation of a faith-based insanity, for such undying forgiveness, a forgiveness that is without end and without expectation, defies any sane measure of logic. It even encourages people like John the Baptist to do irrational things like living on locusts in the desert.

Faith-based insanity is captured, I think, in our abiding love for our children. This faith allows us to raise a child despite all the evidence in the world that we can't. It allows us to open our arms when we know they may be broken, along with our hearts. It helps us stay up all night waiting for them, with little more than a prayer for their safe return. And it is in this way, I decided, that perhaps a loving God is reaching out to us—maybe even to me.

It took me another six years to work up the courage to join Inquiry. But the seeds were planted in that first year of parenthood. Faith amid doubt. If we could raise angels without any qualifications whatsoever, then maybe I could climb gingerly down from my fence and begin to seek a path to God—without a clue as to where I might be going. So, with a small dose of faith-based insanity, I have chosen to enlist in the Rite of Christian Initiation of Adults program. The invitations are, thus, sent. The journey begins. And I attempt a fumbling prayer for the first time in years.

CHAPTER 2

First Meeting

ifteen "candidates" enter Room A, just down the hall from the chapel. A ring of chairs surrounds a small table. On the table are twelve candles and a bowl of water. A lively, thin woman named Karen Miller enters the room and opens our evening session with a simple song.

This is our room / These are our lives[1]....

We have begun.

Every Tuesday night for the next nine months, we will gather in this way and open with this song, in preparation for a kind of conversation with God and with ourselves. We are not sure how, or even if, this conversation may lead to conversion, least of all me. I have a lot of converting to do, a lot of baggage to be rid of, before God and the entire Catholic Church can squeeze themselves into my heart and soul.

Introductions

Five of us are preparing for baptism. Another three were baptized in Protestant faiths and are looking to become Catholics. Two people left the church entirely, some with great anger, and are cautiously considering a return. One woman is approaching a difficult conversion from the Mormon faith, a decision her parents do not know about. And one soul, me, was baptized but unchurched. We range in age from 23 on up, and our stories are as varied as our eventual destinations. But we have chosen this room to begin. Over the course of many years, many discussions with loved ones, and too much soul-searching for any mere mortal, we have decided to take this first tiny step in a potentially wonderful and wrenching journey. We are headed down this slippery slope on a two-thousand-year old road that began, I suppose, when John the Baptist first dunked Jesus in the river.

Karen welcomes the group. She introduces six volunteers who will act as guides and facilitators in our weekly meetings. Then she gives special thanks to a group of people called sponsors. These are friends, and sometimes strangers, who have volunteered to serve as personal mentors for each of the RCIA inquirers. All in all, there are nearly two leaders for every follower. I guess this is a pretty good ratio, considering the path before us.

Eventually, Karen describes the program that will consume much of our attention until spring. We will meet every Tuesday evening to explore the meaning of a relationship with God and the Church. Our sponsors will attend sporadically, but we're encouraged to meet with them on our own time to ask questions and share doubts. We're asked to keep a journal, and to record pretty much anything and everything. Then, a month before Easter, we'll be asked to sign our name into a big book that demonstrates our commitment to conversion. That ceremony is called the Rite of Enrollment, and it will mark the third decision in my Big Leap of Faith. At that point, the show kicks into high gear. Those people who sign the Book of the Elect will meet and be blessed by the local bishop. Our group will go on a retreat of prayer and reflection. Then, on the Saturday before Easter Sunday, during the Easter Vigil Mass, we will take center stage and be welcomed into the Catholic Church.

Whew!

I gaze around the room at the other inquirers, and see them doing mental gymnastics. How will they fit all this into their schedules? Is this more than they'd bargained for?

Karen assures us we can handle it. We're beginning one of the great journeys of our life, one that will change us forever, and all great journeys take time. We believe her.

Conversion Road Map

Karen closes the meeting by asking our sponsors to light the candles and place them in the hands of each candidate. While Karen plays the guitar, we kneel before the bowl of water and place the lit candles on the surface. Their light against the darkened room is simple and serene.

Open my eyes, Lord. / Help me to see your face²....

As we stand in the circle, with the music playing, the six volunteers distribute a card to each of us. On one side is a stencil of a cross and on the other is something she calls the Nicene Creed. I quickly glance over the words and know that I have heard them many times. Almost every week, the priest will lead the congregation in reciting this creed. To be honest, I haven't paid much attention. It was like a code or password the Catholics around me knew from birth. Sitting comfortably on my fence, there seemed no need to know the code. But now that I am standing before this threshold of faith, it's clear that the Creed is a road map for conversion. If I can accept these words, then I am a Christian and am well on my way to becoming a Catholic; if I can't, then I am not ready after all! The clarity is freeing, really. The Church does not want a muddied or hesitant conversion. It wants believers.

Once home, I tape the Creed into my journal so I can check, again and again, my own questions against the answers of the Church, to see if we are to be joined after all.

We believe in one God,
the Father, the Almighty,
maker of heaven and earth,
of all that is seen and unseen.

We believe in one Lord, Jesus Christ,
the only Son of God,
eternally begotten of the Father;
God from God, Light from Light,
true God from true God,
begotten, not made, one in Being with the Father.
Through him all things were made.
For us and for our salvation
he came down from heaven:

by the power of the Holy Spirit
he was born of the Virgin Mary, and became man.

For our sake he was crucified under Pontius Pilate;
he suffered, died, and was buried.

On the third day he rose again
  in fulfillment of the Scriptures;
he ascended into heaven
  and is seated at the right hand of the Father.
He will come again in glory to judge the
  living and the dead,
and his kingdom will have no end.

We believe in the Holy Spirit, the Lord,
  the giver of life,
  who proceeds from the Father and the Son.
  With the Father and the Son he is worshiped
    and glorified.
  He has spoken through the Prophets.
  We believe in one holy catholic and
    apostolic Church.
  We acknowledge one baptism for the
    forgiveness of sins.
We look for the resurrection of the dead,
  and the life of the world to come. Amen.

This is a lot to accept, and I seriously consider giving up. Then I make myself a promise: In the course of the next nine months I will address each statement, each layer of commitment embodied in the Creed, so that my conversion is made with open eyes. I do believe that if I can apply these ancient words to my own long-standing questions and doubts, then my journey will be worth the effort, regardless of the outcome.

CHAPTER 3

One God

We believe in one God,
the Father, the Almighty...

K aren hands a slip of paper to each of the candidates in the room. On the paper is a question of
faith. We are expected to sit quietly, write our answers, and then gather into small groups for discussion.

Initially, I not only had reservations about this journey, I also was not thrilled about discussing it with strangers. What if the leader was a bible thumper? What if the
other candidates were glassy-eyed converts-to-be? After
a month, however, I confess that I enjoy these sessions. I
imagine that the early Christian communities began this
way—gathering in small groups, asking large questions.
During the hurly burly of the week, with work and family, these meetings keep me centered. The discussions are
helping frame my view of the world.

Imaging God

This week's note reads: *Describe your image of God.*

During our small group discussion, Jillian, who is now a Lutheran, says that try as she might, she is stuck with her childish image of God: an old man seated behind an ornate desk full of papers and quills, handing out orders to a host of angels by his side. David, who is looking over the rather low fence of the Episcopal church into the Catholic field, says God is more a sound than an image—like the noise of the ocean from inside a large conch.

As with most of Karen's writing assignments, this one seems harmless on the surface. But, for me, this simple request lies at the heart of everything. Who is this God? Does God have one face, or one sound, or many? How will I know? Evidently, the question was central to the early Church as well, for it ranks number one on the list of critical beliefs in the Nicene Creed.

Uber-God?

Earlier in the month, Karen discussed the history of the Nicene Creed. I didn't hear it quite the way she told it, of course. One never does. But the gist of the story is that creeds, as a general rule, are created, debated, and written down largely as a reaction to something else. The creators feel compelled—or sufficiently threatened—to distinguish their beliefs in contrast to those of another group; to say, in effect, *our* beliefs are "truth," not *yours*. The Catholic Church has several of these creeds—which says as much as anything about its long, and at times contentious history.

In the first or second century after Jesus' death, the leaders of a young and still undefined Church wrote the Apostles' Creed, which formed the basis for the Nicene Creed two hundred years later. At the time, the early leaders were arguing with a group of people, called the Gnostics, who believed that Jesus merely embodied the Spirit of God. In other words, he was *not* God or the Son of God. When Jesus died, the Spirit left him to return to God, and, as such, the Gnostics did not believe in the Resurrection. They did not believe in a number of things, but the Gnostics would not be too uncomfortable with my teenage view of God as Enlightened Force. Obviously, the Apostles' Creed had a lot of ground to cover, and it begins with the first statement. **We believe in one God, the Father, the Almighty....**

Some religious scholars believe this phrase is a direct response to a Christian from Asia Minor called Marcion. Marcion believed there was a Creator-God of the Old Testament who was rigid and vengeful, and who created both good and bad things. Then there was a true *uber*-God, the God of the New Testament, who was the source of love and life. The authors of the Creed confronted this heresy head-on by stating, unequivocally, that there is *only one God*. In other words, the authors figured they had to begin with the basics.

Since I have a lot of ground to cover, this is naturally where I begin too, for this is what finally compelled me to climb down from the fence. I believe there is one God, but God has many faces.

The ancient tribes of Africa, and the ancient Greeks and Romans, for that matter, could not imagine only one God. They saw, instead, a refraction of God's face, as if gazing into a crystal chandelier. They could not see the light, but only fragmented aspects of the source. The ancients of the world were not so much heathens, as they are often called, as they were incomplete in their vision. They saw glimpses of God in fire and rain, in life and death. Their mistake was in believing that each was a god unto itself.

Finding God's Face

When Jillian sees God behind a desk or David hears God as the ocean, they are not heathens precisely because they recognize the incompleteness of their vision. But they were not afraid to describe that image. They spoke their truth as they saw it, knowing full well that God was well beyond their powers of description. And no one laughed or mocked.

So I took my paper, with the impossible request on one side, and flipped it over. On the blank paper, I drew a wheel, and at the center of the wheel, I drew a hub. I labeled the hub God. From the outside to the inside, I drew six spokes. That was my image.

"Each spoke," I explained to my small group, "is a path to God." I showed them the Protestants and the Catholics, the Jews and the Muslims, the Hindi and the Buddhists all residing at each end of a spoke. These groups all faced the same direction: toward God.

David looked at the drawing. "So, God is a hubcap."

Or a sun. Or a marble. In the end, I suppose, the actual image doesn't matter. The point is to face God, even if we can't see a face. Then, like so many others on this Wheel of Faith, we must travel down the spoke toward the center, as far as the path leads—or as far as our faith will allow.

That, to me, is the importance of one God: It makes locating one's faith a lot easier.

CHAPTER 4

Behind Good and Evil

...maker of heaven and earth,
of all that is seen and unseen...

What is *behind* good and evil? Is the devil pushing evil in the world? Is God pulling strings for goodness? These questions matter, for they frame our approach to life. They mark the difference between hope and despair, between whether we've got a decent chance to deal our future, or whether the cards are out of our hands—and in the hands of sources we cannot see but can only fear. I've looked for answers to these questions, from Zen to Nietzsche. So it was pretty surprising to find enlightenment on a movie date. It was even more surprising to finally see its significance in the Nicene Creed.

Penance for Heaven

With evil and terror paraded on the nightly news, I have to wonder if there is some force that compels the terrorists and wife-beaters of the world to the Dark Side. Does Satan prowl the planet and draw the weak and the afflicted? Are we in a kind of spiritual warfare between good and evil? Have we always been?

This question of good versus evil has been argued ever since we could ask questions. The Gnostics believed the universe was inherently evil. Moreover, they believed that God, the true *uber*-God, did not create it. Why, they argued, would a loving God create such a nasty place? In fact, the Gnostics taught that the best way to reach God was to reject this rotten world. Diligent learning, meditation, and a lot of prayer would bring us to God. In short, we were born into a bad place and we had to earn our way out. Nirvana isn't for the weak-minded.

But to me, the process seemed too much like spiritual positioning, like paying penance to some great Gatekeeper in the sky who alone can reveal the secret password into heaven. When I was in high school, I began to explore these so-called paths to enlightenment. Since Gnosticism was then too close to Christianity for me, I took a more Eastern tack: Zen Buddhism.

For Want of a Hip Joint

In retrospect, Zen was simply my quest for God without saying the G-word, which was frowned on in my family. It was spirituality for intellectuals—or wannabes like me.

What is the sound of one hand clapping?

Emptiness, not holiness, is the gift of Buddha.

These *koans* opened my mind to a spiritual universe I never knew existed. In other words, they were confusing enough to seem cool. In fact, Zen has parallels to Gnosticism. Several of the early Gnostics were trained in

India, where Buddhism was founded. Both philosophies seem to point away from the world and toward some inner sanctum of peace. Thus, in a convoluted way, Zen represented my first step toward Christianity—even if it *was* the Gnostic kind.

In the end, however, Zen never seemed to answer its own questions. The Zen Masters proclaimed Enlightenment as an end unto itself. But enlightenment of *what*, I always wondered? Me? God? And the process of getting there, wherever "there" was, involved so much denial of the external world around me and so much inner meditation that I couldn't keep pace. To be honest, I couldn't keep my legs crossed either. So, for want of a decent hip joint, I was forced to seek another path to God.

That was when I found Nietzche—the man remembered for saying, "God is dead." Talk about a confused teenager! His most famous book, *Beyond Good and Evil,* presents "good" and "evil" merely as concepts made up by weak-minded people to explain the world: If God doesn't exist, then neither does Satan—nor much of anything else, for that matter.

Well, this was mighty interesting stuff, but it didn't exactly make me want to sing for joy, much less climb down from my spiritual fence.

Out of Africa, Into the Light

Almost ten years later, Meri helped bring me to ground. Even then, it took a big fight before I had my own glimpse at this thing called "enlightenment." The night began harmlessly, with dinner and a movie, *Out of Africa.* Yet, at evening's end, we'd seen two different films—and exposed something far deeper in the bargain. I saw the character of Denys Finch-Hatten flying his biplane away from the dirty earth of Africa, in an endless quest for freedom. Meri focused on Isak Dinesan digging into the earth of her failing farm, and trying to claim both it and the man she loved. As our fight gained momentum—and importance—we realized that it wasn't just our view of the movie, but of the world, that was in debate.

In essence, Meri reflected the view of the Church she was raised in: The world is good and we need to be engaged in it. No inward escapism. No flying away. The early Church could not have agreed more. That's why, at several points in the Nicene Creed, the authors emphasize this message. *...maker of heaven and earth, of all that is seen and unseen.* (and again later) ***Through him all things were made.*** Very clearly, the early Christians are stating that God made everything—not *most* things, not just the *good* things, but *all* things. Moreover, if one goes back to Genesis, all those things "were good." That includes the light *and* the dark.

Evil, then, is not so much the push of the devil, but the result of the rejection of God. People manufacture evil because they've lost, or had stolen from them, the inherent goodness of God—the goodness that is their birthright and that I felt so clearly in the delivery room at the births of our own two children.

Best of Intentions

Last night, at RCIA, we had a little debate. While in one of our breakout sessions with three other people, I mentioned a quote I'd found in the New Testament. At the time, I was looking for loopholes, which I will ashamedly discuss in the next chapter. But what I found seemed to sum up this complex relationship between God, people, good, and evil. It comes from the short Third Epistle of John (verse 11b). "Whoever does good is from God; whoever does evil has not seen God."

We were talking about good intentions and whether they ever did anybody any good, when I said, "See, even if the person only intends to do good, he is acting with God. But the person who intends and does evil is not necessarily acting with Satan. He or she simply hasn't seen God, and is acting without God."

You should have seen the ruckus that started!

Sam is a Baptist construction manager. He said, "Don't fool yourself. Adam and Eve didn't just decide to sin because they hadn't seen God in a while. They were tricked into it by Satan in the form of a snake." Christina, who is marrying a Catholic two months after our Easter ceremony, said, "I always thought the greatest sin was when they hid from God." And David, my friend who heard God in a conch, laughed and said our intentions didn't seem to matter either way since the road to hell is paved with good ones.

Eventually, Karen called us back to the main group and we returned our chairs to the center of the room. We never did resolve our differences, but that seemed to be fine with everyone. James Joyce once famously described the

Catholic Church as "Here comes everybody." There's room in the Church for sinners and saints, and even naïve folks like me. But I still think I have the weight of evidence, and it can be found in every delivery room. It is the Godliness in the creation of all people, not just the "good" ones.

Taste and See

At its core, Christianity is a positive religion. It speaks of hope and redemption, and it's engaged in this world. God inspired it, and provided the spiritual muscle to make it all happen. Creation is God's gift, a good gift, and we do ourselves a favor when we engage in it.

When Meri and I lived in Washington, D.C., we attended a church on the campus of Georgetown University. It was a fairly small Mass that was celebrated at Dahlgren Chapel, but the community was vibrant and the homilies were inspiring—even to a non-believer like me. My favorite moment came just before everyone marched to the front of the church to receive Eucharist. A woman stood before the choir and sang "Taste and See," the most beautiful Communion song I have ever heard.

She sang this simple song over and over again as the congregation stepped up in line, hands cupped, to taste the bread and wine and to see Christ's face. At this church, even the non-believers walked with the others, our hands crossed over our chests to signal we would not be dining that morning, thank you, and received instead a simple blessing from the priest. It was always at that moment, with that angelic voice calling for people to come and see, that I felt a kindred spirit with my other churchgoers. Even as an outsider, I loved their earnestness.

I could not believe then what they believed, but I felt something that went far beyond appreciation, almost to indebtedness, that there, in the midst of every chaotic and sometimes hellish thing this world has to offer, these people were choosing to see the goodness in this place, the goodness in all of its creation. This, to me, is one the finest aspects of Christianity. In this way, Christianity gives us hope for the world, and for our place in this good place.

CHAPTER 5

A Face and a Prayer

God from God, Light from Light, true
God from true God, begotten, not made,
one in Being with the Father.

At 6:15 in the morning, my room begins to shake violently. I sit bolt upright in bed and stare at my walls, bookshelves, and small desk rumble as though they were perched atop a giant electronic toothbrush. I close my eyes and do the most instinctive thing I can imagine. I pray. "Please, God, make it stop. Please, God, make it stop!"

After a few seconds, the world does stop shaking. The silence is startling. My mother races into the room, gives me a desperate hug, and rushes me downstairs to join the rest of our family. It is Pasadena, California and I am ten years old.

If you had asked me then if I believed in a God who answers prayers, I probably would have wondered what you wanted. Then I would have said, "No, I don't think so...I don't know." Not very profound, I admit, but I was only ten. So who was I praying to? And what about now, if I awoke in my own house, with my own family, to another major earthquake? Thirty years later, I'm ashamed to admit that my beliefs have evolved precious little.

Looking for Loopholes

I take out the Nicene Creed from my RCIA journal and move on to the second stanza. It begins with the longest sentence of the entire Creed and, at thirty-seven words, is devoted to what, for me, has been one very complex subject: the relationship between God and Jesus Christ. The Creed states quite clearly that Jesus is the Son of God and that the two are indivisible. *God from God, Light from Light, true God from true God, begotten, not made, one in Being with the Father.*

God and God's son are one? That is a big leap of faith. In the past, I avoided this subject altogether. Even now, the relationship flies so much in the face of logic that it's easier to turn away. But in the RCIA, there are no detours. So I've been doing a lot of reading lately, with what, I shamefully admit, is not a very lofty goal. Besides the fact that this guilt suggests I am already a Catholic, the truth is that my intentions have not been noble. I've been trying to find a loophole. I've been looking for a respected, religious scholar who could help me to explain away this inconceivable notion. Maybe the concept was simply a test by the founders of the Church to gauge the gullibility of their flock. Maybe the early leaders were assessing the religious market—assuming that if potential converts could believe this, they'd believe anything.

What I discovered was, of course, the opposite.

Liar, Lunatic, Savior

In fact, the books are disarmingly clear about this relationship. Jesus and God are one. My favorite explanation comes from that great writer for adults and children, C.S. Lewis. His point is that people who believe Jesus was simply a great man with a strong religious bent, nothing more and nothing less, are not paying attention. Lewis reminds us that if we read the Bible with any degree of attention, we realize that Jesus himself was quite clear: He states over and over again that he is the Son of God, and moreover, that he and God are one. What Lewis argues is that if you don't believe this, then you cannot also believe that Jesus Christ was a great man. Instead, you must conclude that he was either a raving lunatic or a liar.

Or you can reach a third conclusion: that Jesus Christ was great precisely because he was telling the truth. Lunatic, liar, or savior? It is impossible to believe *all* sides of the argument, because Jesus' proclamations were so clear. And since I do not believe that Jesus was crazy or a liar, the distinct possibility arises that he was telling the truth.

I still don't understand how this works. Apparently, our friends the Gnostics didn't either. They believed Jesus was filled with the presence of God only after his own enlightenment. That's what I had believed. In short, I figured that he, like me, had to "earn" it. Which brings me back to the question of prayer.

Prayer Quota

I remember a conversation with some good friends, a married couple on the Protestant side of the tracks. Nancy was describing another hectic day, schlepping two children around town during the day and serving as an emergency room nurse at night. She suddenly realized, as she was driving home after midnight, that she'd lost her wallet. She could have left it in a dozen different places and had no idea where it might be. Immediately, she prayed—not to be stopped by the police, and for her wallet to be found. When she arrived home, without incident, she found a note from her husband. Lo and behold, a shoe store where she'd been that day had found the wallet and would hold it for her. Her prayers were answered!

"Now, wait a minute," I said. "Do you mean to tell me that God answered your prayers? God was pulling strings in heaven to find your wallet?"

"Why not?"

"That's like when my grandmother would pray for a parking spot. We always laughed at her."

"Did she get a spot?" Nancy asked.

Now this is a question I'd honestly never considered. It was the ludicrousness of her requests that we'd sneered at. "I don't know. Sometimes, I suppose."

"Then sometimes, I suppose, God answered."

In remembering the conversation now, I think what really bothered me was that Nancy and my grandmother were not taking these requests seriously enough. Even as a devout agnostic, I believed that a greater spiritual power could intervene in the world, but only on special occasions, when

the request was very important, like during an earthquake.
In other words, God was like the CEO of the universe and
we were God's lowly staff. Every now and then, we could
ask a favor—but not too often or we'd risk a demotion or,
worse, being handed a really bad assignment. To put it another way, we had a prayer quota.

In one of my children's favorite videos, *Elmo's Christmas,* Elmo—the furry red Sesame Street creature with the
cute laugh—is given three wishes. For his first wish, he asks
for a glass of water. Instantly, one appears in his hand. But
his friends cannot believe the stupidity of this request. "You
wasted a wish on a glass of water? How could you do that?"

Elmo answers, "I was thirsty."

For those of you scoring at home, Elmo's other two
wishes were for Christmas to occur every day; and, finally,
to reverse the second wish when he realized he was killing
Sesame Street with too much of a good thing. Which goes to
show that the first wish wasn't so stupid after all.

The point, however, is that I believed I had about three
or four prayers allocated to me, max, and they had better be
good ones. Like for world peace.

In this light, seeing Jesus as God has come as quite a
revelation. It changes the prayer equation. Jesus as human
makes God that much more approachable, like a friendly
adult with all the answers. You just need to prod him a little.
But for me it goes deeper, in part because now, after all these
years, I can see a face for God. I now understand that God is
everywhere and has many faces—too many for us to know
all of them. But what an approachable face Jesus has—the
kind of face one might pray to, and even get an answer.

CHAPTER 6

Creation and the Body Snatchers

Through him all things were made.

A t 8:00 in the morning, I find myself seated before a chrome and Formica™ table at the House of Waffles. It is a strange place for a benediction.

Fear Factor

I order waffles, of course, and begin the first independent meeting with my sponsor since I entered the RCIA program two months ago. Before entering RCIA, I asked Doug to be my sponsor for two reasons: He is an understanding friend; and, almost as significant, he completed the RCIA program just last Easter. Having "passed" with flying colors, he says that receiving Eucharist for the first time was the most amazing experience since the birth of his second child. I am over-awed at even the thought of duplicating that moment.

I asked Doug to meet me this morning to help me through a religious obstacle. I seem to be facing them with alarming frequency. This one begins at "the beginning"—with Genesis. During a recent evening at RCIA, Karen Miller had given out another of her seemingly simple questions: "What is preventing you from having a closer relationship with God?" I could list several: lack of religious experience, which has made it hard to recognize God; lack of time to grow that experience; and, of course, the "fear factor." Sometimes I feel like the last hold-out in that truly creepy movie, *The Invasion of the Body Snatchers*. I feel like God and God's minions are coming to get not just my soul, but also my brain—that once I cross over to the other side, my mind will become mush. I will stop questioning the world and sit passively in my pew, reciting prayers and creeds with the other Christians.

Church and Science

My father is an eye surgeon and my mother was a practicing nurse. To them, science is truth; everything else is mere conjecture. They are agnostics on a good day and atheists on all the others. And nowhere is this clash more apparent than in the story of creation, when ***Through him all things were made.***

The Bible presents two versions of the creation story. The first claims that God made heaven and earth and all that is seen and unseen in six days and rested on the seventh. The second account focuses on the Garden of Eden and our first Big Mistake. When I was a child, my family read these stories with some amusement, for how could such myths compete with the facts of carbon-dating and Jurassic fossils? It never occurred to me that God and I might have different ways of measuring time.

Doug sets me straight. He directs his gaze over the Belgian waffles and reminds me that he is an electrical engineer and a critical thinker. He uses his brain. Then, of all things, he cites the Bible.

Genesis, he asserts, is scientifically plausible. The story illustrates quite accurately how the universe and the earth may well have been formed: an explosion of light in a formless void; the separation of the waters; the formation of land out of the water. Scientists would count the days in hundreds of millions of years, but the progression of events is the same. Then Doug reveals something that, in my own ignorance, is truly shocking: The Catholic Church does not reject the theory of evolution.

Sure enough, in 1996 Pope John Paul II stated that the theory of evolution is "more than just a hypothesis." At the same time, he reaffirmed that the human soul is created by God only and is "not subject to the evolutionary process." The Catholic Church also warns against biblical literalism. In other words, according to the late Archbishop of Hartford, John Whelan: The Bible is not a science book, is not interested in science, and should not be read as if it were a scientific book. We go to the Bible for religion. We go to scientific studies to learn about the natural sciences.

Well, I thought, this is certainly not my mother's Catholic Church!

My Mother's Church

For my mother, the Catholic Church of her childhood was a dead end, so much so that—after living for nearly three decades according to a litany of Catholic rules that made no sense to her, going to church services that had no meaning for her, and following the seemingly empty rituals of her own Irish Catholic mother—she left. As a final act of filial piety, she did have me and my younger sister and brother baptized. But within a few years she had dismissed organized religion altogether, and has rarely looked back since.

In retrospect, her timing was ironic. At the time of her furious departure, the Catholic Church was undergoing the most profound organizational and social transformation since the Reformation—something called the Second Vatican Council. I had heard about Vatican II, which convened from 1962 to 1965, but it had no meaning for me. To me, Vatican II was simply a bunch of bishops gathering in Rome to finish the work of Vatican I, which had defined "papal infallibility" before its 92-year adjournment in 1870. But after breakfast with Doug, I must admit that I felt mighty ignorant. So I went where any twenty-first century male goes to privately ask for directions: the Internet. After sifting through about a hundred Web sites, my perspective on Vatican II changed. To cite a few examples:

- Mass went from back-turned priests reciting in Latin to celebrations *with* the community and in its local language.
- The Catholic Church opened doors to everything from new music in the service to a more open attitude toward other faiths.
- The Council suggested that non-Christians are open to salvation if they seek God sincerely—for the "divine action of the Holy Ghost is not confined within the limited boundaries of the visible Church."

- And, on a personal level, Vatican II resurrected an ancient practice for the conversion of early Christians and called it the Rite of Christian Initiation of Adults.

In other words, Vatican II not only returned the Church to its people, it declared an openness to all people who seek God.

In reading about these changes, I was stunned. They meant that the Church my family had been railing against for years no longer existed. Certainly, many issues remain, and cries for change (as well as for return) are heard everywhere there are people. But the distinction that I had assumed—between brains and religion—is false. The choice between passive piety and an active, questioning faith simply isn't valid. The Church does not proclaim a deadbolt lock on knowing God's methods, including Creation itself, or God's will. The Church, collectively, asks questions.

Perhaps this was always the case, on some level. Just as the Apostles' and Nicene Creeds defined a new Church, Vatican II *redefined* an old one—and helped return the Church to its more populist roots in the process.

In that process, I also discovered something: that a more open community of Catholics could have a place for people like me. Doug's benediction, then, was the blessing to walk the path to God with my eyes open.

In this sense, all of creation may be God's benediction to us. The earth and the stars are God's blessing. But if God does have a plan, and I imagine God surely must, then creation is more than just a nice place to be: it is our motivation, even our inspiration to keep our collective eyes open and our minds alert while we seek God's grace.

CHAPTER 7

Heaven Is
Where the Heart Is

For us and for our salvation
he came down from heaven.

I now sit in the second row during Mass, up front with my friends in the RCIA, waiting to be called out. At every Mass during the entire nine months of RCIA, we have repeated the same pattern: The presiding priest delivers the homily, and then asks the catechumens and candidates to stand before the congregation. At first, I had to look around to see what one looked like. Eventually, I realized everyone was staring at me and my companion faith-seekers.

"Catechumen" comes from the scriptural phrase: "Those who are taught the word [*ho katechoumenos* in Greek, *is qui catechizatur* in Latin] must share in all good things with their teacher [*to katechounti* in Greek, *ei qui catechizat* in Latin] " (Galatians 6:6). Seems a tad confused, but apparently the concept was quite popular in the early Church. By A.D. 200, prospective Christians were required to participate in a kind of training course to be sure they were ready for the rights and responsibilities as full members of the Church. Some historians believe the training was used as a screening device as well, a good way to weed out Roman spies and Gnostics who might undermine a still fragile institution. I know I need a lot of instructing in all good things, and so here I sit, waiting to go.

Today, the priest finishes a homily about the ascension of Jesus into heaven. Before the eucharistic table is prepared, our class is dismissed from the assembly. This makes sense. If we can't eat the meal, then why endure the preparation of the food? It's like when I steer my children to the special check-out aisle in a grocery store, the one where the candy has been removed to reduce temptation. No need to torture the little dears if they're not getting the sweets—and they're not. We're not either.

The priest directs the congregation to extend their hands over us for a blessing. It's a little embarrassing to be blessed by so many strangers, but this makes sense as well. They seem proud to have us at their gate. They want us to enter their house. I bow my head to accept their blessings, then leave with the rest of the RCIA class to talk about heaven.

Pie in the Sky

We enter one of those "temporary" one-room trailer-like buildings that has become, over the years, permanent. Karen is not with us this morning, so we are led by another facilitator named Susan. It is easy to see, after four months on this journey, why the RCIA requires so many guides. Conversion is a big job.

Susan is a teacher in her daily life, and she lives by posted signs and sticky notes. The room is filled with broad flip-chart paper that has been attached with masking tape to its walls. On one paper, she has written the lines of a familiar song about heaven, *Michael, Row the Boat Ashore*. Susan asks us to come up with other song lyrics, and we are happy to oblige. David, my favorite contrarian, goes first, with a line from a Talking Heads song, "Heaven is a place where nothing ever happens."[3] Susan grimaces, and then writes the line on a sheet of paper with a magic marker. Amy, our struggling Mormon member, gives an old reggae tune from Jimmy Cliff that is not very flattering either—about waiting for pie in the sky when we're all suffering here on earth. Even John Lennon's *Imagine* is of a perfect world where there's no heaven at all. Susan seems less than pleased with our images. That's pop culture for you! She asks us to continue, and we come up with more conflicting pictures of heaven—as sweet, or boring, or simply unattainable.

In the end, we don't make much progress, but the exercise does reveal a common thread: Though we talk a lot about it, no one really knows this place called heaven.

Heaven in a Jug

Over the past couple months, I've developed a running correspondence with the pastor of our church. Every now and then, I send him offbeat questions by e-mail, and he responds with straight answers. I've asked him about evil, and God's plan for us, and his answers are sprinkled throughout this book. I recently sent the pastor a question about the nature of heaven. His response suggests that I am not alone in my "unique" images for God or creation or even heaven.

To paraphrase, my pastor's analogy is of a heaven full of jugs and vats of various shapes and sizes. The jugs embody our own capacity to be filled with the spirit and love of God. We create the jugs on earth by the way we live our lives and approach God. Some jugs are large and simple, such as an earthenware vase one might find with a Franciscan monk, or during the time of Jesus. Others might be detailed and ornate, carved by the owner's love of religious tradition and doctrine. But what is most important—to us, the creators of these "earthen vessels"—is that when we do enter heaven, our jugs will all be full. No matter the size or the shape, we will be filled with God's grace. In other words, heaven will reflect what we have imagined it to be on earth. If we are full of God's love here, in whatever form, we are sure to be full of that love in eternity.

I kind of like the image. There are others, of course: clouds of angels, an oasis in the sky. I even have one unfortunate vision of a steam room, from a play I saw, where the recently dead wait in bath towels for admission to heaven and God plays practical jokes on the poor souls of earth.

In the end, maybe it doesn't matter. The Nicene Creed doesn't seem to fixate on the place where Jesus came from, only on the fact that he came.

Heaven in the Back Row

After talk of heaven and Susan's disapproving looks, I get permission to leave the RCIA session early. I receive this "special dispensation," to use a Catholic term, because a family friend is giving a "faith sharing." This is when a member of the congregation stands at the ambo at the end of Mass and tells us how faith changed his or her life. I know I could use a few pointers. Yet, what I hear is far better, for my friend Carol has actually seen this place called heaven.

Carol is a woman of fire and light, and opens with the illness of her son. Stephen has spinal muscular atrophy (SMA), a debilitating condition that has put him in a wheelchair for life. SMA is a rare genetic disease, characterized by wasting of the skeletal muscles, which causes weakness and atrophy of the voluntary muscles. Doctors had targeted his life span at five, and then ten. Stephen is now eleven. He is a bright, lively boy who is charming and tenacious. A year ago, he had his spine fused to keep him from breaking his back, since he could not support his increasing body weight. The operation strengthens the spine, but it also means he will not grow another inch. So when Carol speaks of illness, she means it. And when she speaks of God, one gets the impression that she's had many conversations.

Last November, my son Stephen came down with a cold. Anyone who knows my son, knows that a cold usually means pneumonia. I took Stephen to the doctors' office after a week of his being sick, but without a fever. The doctor decided the best thing to do was simply watch him. After another two weeks, Stephen still did not have a fever, but he didn't get any better either. So I took him back to the doctor. This time I got quite a different response. The doctor took one look at Stephen, put him on oxygen, and told the nurse to call 911. I wasn't able to accompany Stephen in the ambulance to the emergency facility because I have three other kids and they were still in school. So I rushed around and made some phone calls to make arrangements for them. Then I packed an overnight bag and endured one of the longest forty-five minute drives of my life, to the Children's Hospital to see my son.

Before continuing Carol's story, it is important for you to know that Stephen was not diagnosed with SMA until Carol was already pregnant with her fourth child. Maggie, still *in utero,* was then also diagnosed with SMA. Both children require constant care with every facet of living. So when one reads "make arrangements" for her other children, one should hear "understatement." In fact, to suggest that life is a struggle for this family would also be an understatement. But to say so would not do them justice, for both parents and all four children are proud, full of joy, and very involved in our community. It probably would be more accurate to say that they inspire us beyond measure.

During the car ride, I thought of many things. I thought about how scared Stephen is of IVs, and how no one is there with him in the hospital. I only hoped the firemen were nice when they took him. I thought about how much I love Stephen, and how empty my life would be without him. And, of course, I thought about what kind of a mother lets her child get sick enough that he needs an ambulance to go to the hospital! As you might imagine, I had several conversations with God as I drove to see Stephen.

When I got to the hospital, Stephen was already better. He was watching cartoons in bed, pretty much like nothing had happened—except for the oxygen and Albuterol™ mask strapped onto his face. Soon it was late, and after Stephen had fallen asleep, I lay down on the window seat with a hospital sheet over my head and fell asleep. I had a dream.

In the dream, a voice asked if I wanted to see heaven and I answered, "Yes, I'd like to see heaven." And so a young man who had been standing in a group of people came forward, and I knew this person was Jesus. I immediately recognized him as someone I had seen before, literally on a daily basis. He was the person who always stood in the back. He had always been in the background of many of my church, school, and social groups. I said to him, "I recognize you," and he said, "Yeah"—like, no kidding—"I know you do."

Now it was time to see what heaven looked like, and Jesus led me forward. Instead of ascending into the sky, he showed me different scenes from my own life. That was my tour. Heaven was on earth. And the funny thing is, I knew I was in heaven all the time. I was in heaven only because I recognized it. And those who didn't know, were not. As I looked around, I wasn't quite sure what to make of this, but at the time it all made perfect sense.

I regained consciousness, this incredible feeling of love came over me. It was the kind of love you feel when you're on your honeymoon, or when you look at old photographs of your children, except that this feeling was even more intense. As I realized I was waking up, I knew the feeling would leave also. I didn't want to leave this feeling. I fought the stirring of my consciousness, but eventually I awoke.

Carol paused. The entire congregation was well into its second tissue to dry the tears. Then she told a story.

I was reminded of that line in Scripture that reads, "Were not our hearts burning within us..." (Luke 24:32). After Jesus had been crucified and laid in the tomb, the disciples were walking on the road to Emmaus when they met Jesus, but they did not recognize him. I always thought that part of the story was odd. Do you think Jesus did this on purpose? Was he testing his friends, or fooling them? Only later, in the breaking of the bread, did they recognize him. It was at this precise moment that the disciples truly saw Jesus for what he was. Through Stephen and my dream, I finally understood this passage. Jesus was saying to them: "No longer will you recognize me through my physical characteristics. From now on, you will recognize me through my actions in your world."

Carol stated that she would not have believed her dream without the love she felt just before she awakened. God is love, and God is in her relationships—even if she had not recognized the Big Relationship standing in the back of the room. To put it another way, when Jesus came down from heaven all those years ago, he must have brought it with him. Both are here, among us, if we can only recognize them.

Heaven on My Mind

An old joke tells of a man who enters heaven. As he is shown the premises, the man points to the Jews over there and the Baptists over here, and then he points to a high wall that is enclosed on four sides. "Why is that wall in heaven?" he asks. "Shh," the guide says, "the Catholics are on the other side. They think they're the only ones here."

The joke could apply to almost any denomination, or religion, and it supports the "jug theory" of heaven. If you live a life of exclusive clubs and gated communities, you will likely find an exclusive heaven of your own design. If you believe in a catholic heaven, in the literal sense of the word, where "here comes everybody," then heaven could be as crowded as a street bazaar. On the other hand, if you long for tranquility on earth, or for people to leave you alone, for God's sake, you may well find that the heaven which awaits you is a vase of your own design, as pristine and smooth as porcelain. Your heaven will be a place where nothing ever happens—and you'll be happy as a clam.

What Carol showed me, inadvertently, was the interactive, participatory side of heaven—not just on our part, but on the part of God. The Nicene Creed speaks of it. *For us and our salvation he came down from heaven.* What Carol suggests is that not only did Jesus come for us—not once, but twice, as a babe and after his death—but he is here now. He is standing in the back of the room. And if Jesus is both here *and* in heaven now, seated at the right hand of God, then perhaps we are in heaven as well, making our vases for eternity. Heaven, quite literally, is what we make it.

Or, to quote another popular "prayer": *Thy kingdom come. Thy will be done, on earth as it is in heaven.*

CHAPTER 8

The Second Step

*By the power of the Holy Spirit he was
born of the Virgin Mary, and became man.*

Growing up, Christmas was a wonderful spectacle. My father over-compensated for his own low-income childhood by lavishing us with gifts. Since both my parents left their respective families and religions far behind when they moved to California, we created our own traditions. So instead of Mass, every Christmas Eve we drove to the bookstore to choose a book, and then drove around town to see the holiday lights. Eventually, we'd return home to open a roomful of family presents, one by one. The next morning, we awoke to more from Santa.

Every year the tradition continued, and grew in abundance. One year stands out because it captures the tension a lot of secular families feel, I think, who try to celebrate what is ultimately a religious holiday. When in ninth grade, I was just learning photography. So, of course, that Christmas I got a dark room set—an enlarger, developer baths, the works. The only trouble was I had to build the room myself. After many attempts with black paint and cardboard, I failed to get the room dark enough and all my prints ended up light-washed and fuzzy. In the end, I was sure that I had failed to live up to the gift.

When I tell friends of this dilemma of excess, they laugh and ask if my parents would adopt them. But in retrospect, it may explain the need to earn my gifts, even those from God. At the same time, I believe my dad simply did not know what else to give, beyond his love and largesse. We were, in effect, speaking past each other, in different languages, wanting different things.

This year, with heaven and the Christ child on my mind in greater urgency, or at least in closer proximity, Christmas itself has changed. I feel a part of something ancient, one with a long line of seekers and believers that dates back two thousand years. This connectedness to God, and to those in the RCIA, has helped me navigate the season. It's grounded me to shore, so to speak, within a sea of holiday hoopla.

Old Ghosts

With the New Year, however, comes a special sense of dread. Easter is less than four months away. We begin to increase speed down that slippery slope toward the moment of truth. No more lofty discussion of heaven, no more safe questions about prayer and creation. Instead, the anxiety of the next step—the second decision—has been rising like bath water in an overflowing tub. And I seem unable to turn off the tap.

If the first step—joining the RCIA program—was hard, at least it was done on home ground. I made the decision as an adult, surrounded by loved ones and a supportive community. The second step is more about trudging on old ground, confronting the old ghosts of family and friends who, for better or worse, made me what I am. Or at least what I was—which finally exposes the real fear of this sea change in my soul.

The problem is not so much that I may be abandoning old ghosts, though that is painful enough, but that I am abandoning *myself*. Even more critically, this is a major departure from the person I always thought I wanted to be. This is perhaps the hardest part: learning to accept the "me" I never intended, the one who believes and accepts and embraces a religion that my family rejected and I was sure I would never need.

It is a journey of a million miles, and it begins with this second step.

A Good Joke

My brother and sister and their spouses are coming tonight, for a little dinner and a confession. It is time to reveal, precisely, what I am doing with my life. What *am* I doing?

I've thought of a thousand subtle ways to raise the delicate subject with my siblings. Over dinner, I could tack the subject on at the end of a series of jokes, like, "Yeah, that's a good one. How about something even funnier? I'm gonna be a Catholic!" Or I could try that old teenage ploy: make this issue seem mild when compared to other worst-case scenarios. "Sis, Bro, I've decided to become a terrorist...Just kidding...I'm only going to be a Christian!" Ultimately, I decide to be subtle: work the subject in casually, as if choosing a faith is the most casual thing in the world.

Well...I Have Something to Tell You

After dinner, we sit around the living room and I wait for a lull in the conversation. I clear my throat. "Well, um, I have something to tell you." That's me—subtle as a train wreck. They stare, because there's not much else to do after such an opening. "Well," I continue, "for the past several months, I've been involved in an RCIA program." I quickly explain what RCIA stands for, and what it means for me. "The people who complete the program are scheduled to join the Catholic Church on Easter, in four months."

My brother, Doug, looks incredulous. "So, does that mean you're becoming Catholic?"

"Well...." I say that there's a good possibility.

My sister, Kyra, gets right to the point. "Do Mom and Dad know?"

"Well...." I say that they will soon. That is the second half and more difficult part of this step, which naturally means it will be postponed. "I think I'll write a letter first, so they can absorb the impact on their own time, and then we'll talk in person."

So far, so good, I think. Then they begin with the questions of faith. They're kind, respectful, and very pointed.

As predicted, they ask if I believe in God. That's an easy one. I tell them that I think I've always believed in God, I was just afraid to give God a normal name—as if Force, or Something Higher were a nickname.

They ask why I'm joining the *Catholic* Church, of all things. This answer is so complicated that I think I'll save it for another chapter. (For the curious, skip ahead to Chapter 13.)

Then they shift into higher gear and ask a series of technical questions, designed, I think, to see where I really stand. One of the toughest, the one we spend the most time on—the one that has always seemed the most ludicrous—concerns the virgin birth. At first, I give the academic argument that "virgin" in Hebrew, the original language of most of the Bible, means "young girl." But we all know what the Catholic position on this is, and that's not it. In fact, the Nicene Creed puts it quite clearly, as always. *By the power of the Holy Spirit he was born of the Virgin Mary, and became man.*

So I try another angle: We discuss "miracles."

God and the Holy Transmitters

Miracles do happen. As someone put it, miracles happen when God mixes with us. Miracles occur at the nexus of people and God; people reach out to God and God reaches out to people. It only seems natural that, when all this potential kinetic energy connects, sparks begin to fly.

With my family listening, I grope for analogies. I ask my siblings if they believe in some Higher Force. I call it Power to keep things safe. My sister does, tentatively; my brother has doubts. If pressed, I believe my parents do—as does most of the world, I think. "Maybe it's like a microwave," I say, "or radiation. You can't see it, but you can see what it does."

"But that's science," says my brother. "You can test for radiation, prove it exists."

"Maybe that's simply because we know how to test for it. A couple centuries ago, we didn't believe in microwaves. A couple decades ago, we didn't believe in quarks, either, but they existed. They always existed, from the beginning. We just didn't understand enough to know they existed. Maybe God is just operating on a different wavelength, one we don't yet understand."

My sister rolls her eyes. "So you're saying God is like some holy transmitter."

"No, not quite. Maybe God is more like a holy generator and we're the transmitters."

The skepticism in the room is rising, so I figure I might as well plow ahead. "That's where the miracles occur: at the point of transmission. If radiation has power and substance and impact, then maybe this Higher Power does too. When we connect to it, great things can happen—sometimes even miracles. If you can acknowledge this Power is real—and I do—then who's to say what it can or cannot do. After all, the Pilgrims never would have believed that a bunch of invisible waves could have prepared their Thanksgiving dinner."

Well, now I've lost them completely, and in a way it's my own fault. I've tried to apply some sort of spiritual logic—which may be an oxymoron—and debate them with reasoning and science because that's what we were taught in our family. But I feel as if I'm simply throwing up smoke and mirrors around my faith.

More to the point, I know my siblings can see it too. They know I'm groping, so I try something that does not come easily: I speak from the heart. It's not easy because the heart does not make sense. The argument doesn't hold because, in reality, there is no argument. In the end, I suppose, faith cannot be argued. It can only be felt. Flailing away at technicalities, I take my humble stand.

"Look," I admit, "I don't have the answers yet. All I know is that when I pray, I feel something. When my children were born, I felt something, and to me it was very real. I felt connected to Something Higher, to that microwave in the sky, to God, after all. And after all these years of hemming and hawing and splitting logical hairs, I've decided to seek the Source. I don't know what else to say except that it feels right."

Then a surprising thing happens. No one laughs or points out the utter fallacy in my argument. Instead, my sister smiles and says, "Okay then." My brother says, "Seems like you know what you're doing," which shows what he knows.

And the only thing I can say is, "Thanks." That's all the blessing I needed.

CHAPTER 9

Step Two-and-a-Half

*For our sake he was crucified under
Pontius Pilate; he suffered, died,
and was buried.*

*God said to Abraham, "Kill me a son"
Abe says "Man, you must be puttin' me on"
God says "No." Abe say, "What?"
God says "You can do what you want, Abe, but
The next time you see me comin' you better run"
Well, Abe says, "Where do you want this killin' done?"
God says, "Out on Highway 61."*[4]

This is one of the oldest stories in the Bible as parodied by one of my favorite songwriters, Bob Dylan. It is a story of trial and redemption and that complex trinity between God, a parent, and a child. Only now, as I struggle to face my own mild version of this trinity, do I appreciate its significance. For me, the lyrics and the story are rooted in a timeless conflict: the conflict between the enormous power our families have over us and the power

God has to change that equation in fundamental ways. This is the story of completing the second step, of telling my parents that—twenty years after leaving their house—I am about to leave home.

Is God Bipolar?

In the biblical story, God tells Abraham to sacrifice his only son as a burnt offering. Contrary to Dylan's version, Abraham does not hesitate. He binds his son, lays him on an altar of wood, and is about to stab the boy with a knife when an angel of the Lord intervenes. The angel tells Abraham to stop this madness, and provides a ram, caught in a thicket, as a more suitable substitute.

The story is harsh, as are most interpretations of it. We are told that God wants us to do God's will, regardless of what we might prefer. We are reminded that a couple thousand years later God did allow God's "only" son to suffer and die for an important mission. And lest anyone forget, the Nicene Creed forces us to face these facts every time we recite the Creed in church. *For our sake he was crucified under Pontius Pilate; he suffered, died, and was buried.*

Historically, the authors may have put this line in to address those troublesome Gnostics. They needed to be reminded, apparently, that Jesus was not merely dead, but really most sincerely dead, and that he was buried. Without this fact of death, the Resurrection could not have occurred, and the Resurrection is precisely what the Gnostics doubted. (We'll deal with this most crucial of all mysteries in the next line of the Creed, in the next chapter.) The point is that between these two passages we see a God who is not about fun

and games. In the first, God leads Abraham to the brink of
his family's destruction—as a test. Later, God sacrifices God's
own son for the sake of a bunch of cowards and ingrates.
Now, that's a tough parent. That's taking brinkmanship to a
new level.

But there is a strange disconnect here. The more I look
at God lately—and I look a lot now—the more I seem to see
God's face, or at least feel God's presence. When I pray now,
I feel a kind of warm wind on my soul. And in church, we
are told of a God with limitless love who is ready to forgive
our sins at the first signs of a truly repentant heart. How
could this same heavenly parent, with such a divine disposi-
tion, be so harsh and imperious—and to someone greatly
loved at that? There's no consistency here. Does God assure
us with love and then test us with tragedy? Does God embrace us one day and, the next, tell us to get down and do
twenty push-ups to prove our virtue? To come straight to
the point, is God bipolar?

And what of Abraham? The lesson he suggests is not
too rosy either. Not only is Abraham tested, but the trick
question involves his family. He becomes the fulcrum in this
God-parent-child relationship, and seemingly must choose
between one or the other. The balance of the scale, apparently, must be tipped toward God or toward Abraham's only
son. Granted, in the end, Abraham and his son received redemption, but *only* after he'd passed the test.

These questions, for me, are not just academic. They are
critical to my faith. I don't think I can trust in a god that is
constantly testing me. If God is to be my rock and my salvation, that rock must be solid—not a being that is present
when I am found worthy and absent when I am not. Makes

me a little leery, truth be told. Makes me a little reluctant to love someone with all my heart, soul, and mind—as Jesus demands of us—when the deal seems to come with contingencies, like my worthiness, or my willingness to reject my own family.

Which brings me to the heart and soul of the matter, for here I am facing a similar, though less dramatic "test." In this case, I seem to be the fulcrum between God and my parents. And, it seems, I can't have both.

God as Parent

Every now and then, Karen invites an outside speaker to our RCIA session. He or she will typically join the group after an opening ritual of song and candle lighting, and then sit in a circle of chairs to give new perspectives on faith or prayer. Last week, Father Mark—a young, dynamic preacher who packs 'em in the pews—spoke about the Bible as history, both God's and ours. According to Father Mark, the Old Testament is full of stories about a powerful God who saves this and smites that; a commanding, even jealous God who protects and punishes with seeming impunity. Read Sodom and Gomorrah and its destruction, or the death and redemption surrounding Noah and the flood, or the miraculous salvation wrought by the parting of the Red Sea, or countless other stories to get the message: When God makes a decision, either for us or against "them," God means business. Father Mark reminds us that these stories also reflect only one view of God, the view of a child toward a parent: all-powerful, seemingly unfair, capable of great wrath and compassion—sometimes all in the same breath. No wonder many of the Bible's passages read like an awe-struck fan who is recounting the triumphs of a favorite hero.

The New Testament presents a God that is more like us, more human—so human, in fact, that God sent God's son to make the point. Through Jesus, we see God as someone with whom we can identify and have a personal relationship. When Jesus gets angry in the Temple, weeps for his friend Lazarus, feels lonely in the Garden of Gethsemane, shows impatience with Peter, and displays a host of other human emotions, we see God, somehow, as innately human. Moreover, this construction makes perfect sense if we are, in fact, made in God's image. And by joining with us on earth, God does not become any less than God always was. Actually, God becomes more—still all-powerful, but also more approachable. As Father Mark suggests, this change in perspective from the Old to the New Testaments parallels the maturing view we have toward our own parents—from all-powerful beings to human beings, with faults and frailties disconcertingly like our own.

In this light, God did not change from Old Testament tyrant to New Testament teddy bear. Rather, *we* changed. God is not bipolar. If anything, we are. It is *we* who are inconsistent.

Keeping the Trinity Intact

OK, then, God is consistent. That's a start in this little trust-building exercise. But consistently what? Harsh? Sadistic? This is still the same God who was willing to rip a family apart as a test of loyalty. Is this a God who would be willing to rip mine as well? Or threaten to sacrifice me like a goat?

During the ensuing Q&A, we discussed the Bible in more detail, particularly the trials and struggles of a long-suffering people. David, our foil, asked why the Old Testament seemed to be so obsessed with floods and wars and plagues and disasters of every kind. Father Mark answered in the best of all possible ways. "Because they happened," he said, "all the time. In fact, they still happen all the time."

That night, while writing in my faith journal, the story of Abraham finally fell into place. Stuff like *that* must have happened all the time as well. And sure enough, according to those great historical records, the Bible and the Internet, human sacrifice was indeed common—so much so that the biblical authors had to condemn the practice several times.[5]

If one reads the story of Abraham and Isaac in context, the threat of sacrifice is not unusual. What is shocking, what really turned the religious heads of the day, is not that God asked Abraham to sacrifice his son. Apparently, all the gods were doing this—a kind of trial by fire, if you will. The shocking thing is that God did *not* make Abraham go through with murder. Instead, God compelled Abraham to step back from the edge of familial suicide. It is by this act that the one true God is distinguished from all the other, false gods that did demand such sacrifices. So God is not only not bipolar, neither does God play brinkmanship. God has no need, and indeed no desire, to resort to such tests.

In the end, the God-parent-child relationship in Abraham's timeless trinity is not an either/or situation. God wants this triad intact, and seems to like the configuration in general. The beauty is in the symmetry of the relationship. Each piece is critical to the foundation of the other: we need God, God needs us. Within the family, God relies on us to perpetuate the human race and the monotheistic faith. Seems terrifically simple in the abstract. But, of course, there is the reality of our own personal trinities.

In my case, one branch of this triad—my parents—does not necessarily acknowledge the existence of the other—God. Makes for an interesting dynamic—a bit like trying to introduce an old friend to a ghost or, in this case, Holy Ghost. Not only can the former not see the latter, but the former thinks you're insane for trying the introduction at all. Still, there is this voice inside me insisting on closure, one way or the other.

Personal Trinity, Timeless Choice

Ultimately, Abraham is the story of an active God who intervenes for our sake, whether we are ready or not. In the Bible, New Testament and Old, this is a highly personal and loving God, even if God's methods seem a little suspect at times. In this sense, God is not unlike our parents. If we are very lucky, these parental figures (whatever the exact legal relationship) are involved in our lives, whether *we* like it or not. They meddle. They muck up our best-laid plans. And even more troubling, they are forever. In one way or another, whether through their lives or through our selective memories of them, our parents define us. We may curse them or praise them, but we can't negate them.

To make matters more complex, the relationship itself is always just that: complex. We've known these people a long time. We know their habits, their likes and dislikes, and just how far we can push before they take away the car keys. I know, for example, that my parents are not going to like this conversion.

On the other hand, I understand that God wants a personal relationship with me. To imagine a personally involved God is actually a bit frightening—like getting another parent. While I love my parents, I don't want omnipresent ones. Far too intrusive, to be honest. I don't live in the same city as my parents, and it always seemed much safer having God in another state too, so to speak—where I could call on or ignore God as necessary.

That is the irony of this picture: God wants a personal relationship with me, while my parents have one—and the latter will not even acknowledge the presence of the former. Must I choose between them? In my new understanding of the story of Abraham and Isaac, I see that there is no "choice" to be made, no "sacrifice" of one or the other. To put it more broadly, if God did not want human relationships to distract us, why are our lives so filled with them? Why would God grant us the gift of family if its only purpose was to serve as a sacrifice, to "test" our commitment to God?

When Meri was pregnant with our second child, I also assumed a false choice. Our hearts had been filled completely by our firstborn son, and I truly could not imagine loving another creature. Our little boy was lively, loving, and all-consuming. My love was locked in on a family of three-only, and I was honestly nervous that, when our second came into the world, I would be distant. I was sure that I could love no other, and thought the new kid on the block would somehow have to "earn" my affections.

But then, naturally, the miracle occurred: within a couple of nano-seconds of Marie's birth, my heart simply got larger.

New Math

God equals love. This is the key to understanding God's relationship with people, and it is something Meri had been trying to drum into my head for years. The new math also explains the instinctive and monumental transformation in the delivery room, and it feeds the changing dynamic in the God-parent-child trinity. The equation is remarkably simple, direct, and very powerful. Both are solid and yet infinite in their capacity. Both are eternal. Both thrive on relationships and, at an intrinsic level, exist for our sake.

The equation is where the full message of the Nicene Creed seems to turn, from an emphasis on heavenly presence—a love ethereal—to personal savior—love in the flesh. If we read the line again, from the top, its says *for our sake he suffered, died, and was buried*. The point is so crucial that the Creed reminds us twice. One line earlier, around this same turning point, the Creed states: *For us and for our salvation he came down from heaven.* In each case, this is the message of a deep and selfless love, one that can only be "equated" through our own parent-child bonds. This is a relationship where the two sides are so intimately tied together that they are ultimately inseparable, regardless of time or distance or any family feuds we might encounter.

Jesus seems to understand this relationship intimately. After teaching the disciples the Lord's Prayer, he taught them something about family as well.

"So I say to you, Ask, and it will be given you; search, and you will find; knock, and the door will be opened for you. For everyone who asks receives, and everyone who searches finds, and for everyone who knocks, the door will be opened. Is there anyone among you who, if your child asks for a fish, will give a snake instead of a fish? Or if the child asks for an egg, will give a scorpion? If you then, who are evil, know how to give good gifts to your children, how much more will the heavenly Father give the Holy Spirit to those who ask him!" (Luke 11:9-13).

Clearly, Jesus understood this most fundamental relationship. No matter what wrath a parent may want to inflict, and I know mine wanted to drop kick me a couple times, their love is innate, instinctual. This is not to say that the parent cannot be wrong, or that the child should not leave the parent to find his or her own way in the world or in faith. It *is* to say that bond will never be broken. The relationship is eternal, whether we like it or not. So this new "equation of the trinity" is consistent, and it is solid, for it is founded in love and anchored in family.

At least I hope so, because the time has come to write a letter.

Steve's First Letter to the Pasadenians

I take a deep breath and tell myself to keep thinking about infinite love, about that solid "trinity" that binds my parents with God despite their intentions. As promised, the plan is to write now, talk later. The result is several pages of what, in retrospect, seems to be largely drivel, but since God was doing most of the writing, I don't complain. The point is made. The letter is sent.

It is certainly not the most articulate letter ever written. It is not confident, like one of Paul's, and not convincing, like one of John's. Nevertheless, I do manage to state that *I believe in God*, and that *I am preparing to join the Catholic Church*. I even promise I will *not become a raving lunatic*, as if that might help. Once the letter is in the mail, I feel a profound sense of freedom and possibility. I don't know where I'm going, exactly, and can't say why I'm going there. But after decades of doubt, I now know which side of the fence I'm on. I know what I'm leaving behind. It is a kind of freedom that can only be found in discovering one's sense of direction.

My parents' reaction? As predicted, there is love and misunderstanding.

My dad cannot understand why I need to join some organization to validate my faith. I explain that I'm not looking for validation, but for a community to nurture that faith. No matter. He's a loner at heart. He thinks religion has little to do with God, just something that gets in the way, really, and I kind of respect that.

My mother is more pointed. She reminds me that I'm an adult and can do whatever I want. Having been wounded herself, however, she can't help but sling one arrow about raising a daughter in this particular church. And I kind of respect that too. But no family is perfect, particularly a huge one with a two thousand year lineage, and the Catholic family seems a welcoming place right now.

More important, however, is that we are not split asunder. In the end, we remain present for one another, just as God remains present: the personal triad and the true Trinity. Both are constant, both are founded in love, and I am now joined to them: to my past, my present, and my future. In short, after twenty years of feeling a bit bipolar myself, or at least of two minds, I am beginning to feel whole again.

The possibilities are limitless.

CHAPTER 10

Dying and Rising in Christ

On the third day he rose again in
fulfillment of the Scriptures;
he ascended into heaven and is seated
at the right hand of the Father.

After six months of RCIA, we are at the biggest question of all, coming—appropriately—on the threshold of Lent. The timing couldn't be better.

The previous month was extraordinarily difficult. The process of redefining one's self always is. When family's involved, it's so much harder. There is so much messiness, so many loose ends. It's not as if one simply gathers up character, relationships, personal history, and core sense of self, like so many unraveled threads, and knits together a new tapestry. The challenge is more akin to rebuilding a strange engine while staring into a mirror. You know it's you in the reflection, and you assume it's an engine in your hands, maybe even a car, but every detail is backwards—and there is no guarantee the thing will run once you're done.

Fundamentally, the great shock is that I am on the verge of calling myself a Christian. Not in a hundred lifetimes would I have dreamed that title for myself. It means that not only do I believe in God, but that Jesus Christ is my savior; that he lived, performed miracles, died, and most amazing of all, rose, and eventually ascended to heaven. It is this last, most amazing part that serves as the birth of Christianity and defines the religion forevermore. Of necessity, then, my own birth and redefinition must begin here as well.

A Time to Die

Karen gathers the group before the Lenten season begins. This season is, for many people, a time of reflection and preparation for the great celebration of Easter—the most significant holiday of the Christian calendar. For me, it's a time of countdown and contained panic, because with the beginning of Lent, the clock starts. As of Ash Wednesday, Lent officially begins and only forty days remain until D-Day—at least as Winston Churchill defined it: Deliverance Day. Moreover, between now and deliverance, I must navigate a sea of activities. Karen lays them out in order.

- **The Rite of Election:** With my wife and my sponsor in the room, I am to sign the Book of the Elect, which publicly confirms my intention to join the Catholic Community. After this point, I am no longer a "candidate" and the non-baptized are no longer "catechumens." Instead, we are to be called the "elect." The ceremony is supposed to be beautiful, and for some reason, is the one that I am most anxious about. I have always considered it the third step in my faith journey.

- **The Blessing of the Bishop**: The Sunday after we sign the Book of the Elect, we join the other "elect" from throughout the diocese at a special ceremony where we are to be blessed by the bishop. In some Catholic communities, the book signing and the blessing occur during the same ceremony. It's a lot to absorb in one sitting, so I'm glad that we're keeping it separate this year.

- **The Rite of the Scrutinies**: The Scrutinies occur between Lent and the Rite of Celebration at the Easter Vigil. The non-baptized receive a kind of exorcism from any darkness and sin they may have in their lives. Since I have been baptized, I will witness the Scrutinies from a distance.

- Finally, **The Celebration of the Sacraments of Initiation—** D-Day—when life and afterlife are changed forever.

The journey begins tonight, as Karen introduces this serious season of Lent by launching an equally serious subject: the idea of death. We are told, as gently as possible, that now we must die; before we can be reborn into anything new, we must let go of all the old trappings. This is nothing new really. Almost every religion encourages some great letting go—of old ways, old obsessions, old fears—before a great self-discovery. Buddhism and "born again" Christianity share a passion for earthly release before spiritual awakening. Caterpillars have done it for ages as well. It is not too surprising then that big change must always be preceded by big change. The question is, how much will it hurt?

Forgive Us Our Selves

Open my eyes, Lord, help me to see your face. / Open my ears, help me to hear.

As the song ends, Karen asks everyone to write a secret on a slip of paper. The secret is an obstacle that must die before we can open our hearts and minds to a personal, loving, and at times overwhelming Jesus Christ. This is a mighty tough topic, as well, so Karen provides suggestions.

The obstacle may be a damaging past relationship that has calcified into bitterness. So we are asked to forgive the relation—and our part in it—and let the bitterness die. The obstacle may be a physical limitation, like SMA, or unsightly blemishes, or any of a million frailties that have come to define us. We are asked to forgive the cause—and ourselves, if necessary—and place the limitation in perspective before God. Or the obstacle may be an addiction, a failure, a loss, or a possession—any of an infinite number of problems that block us, in pure and simple terms, from accepting love. We are asked, once again, to forgive ourselves and let the obstacles die.

There is, of course, a pattern here. The key and the challenge is that we are asked to forgive ourselves *before* we can be rid of that which we need to forgive. Not an easy task. It is indeed ironic that the one thing we crave—love—requires the one thing that we already possess: the power of *self*-forgiveness. And this is often the one thing we deny ourselves. Why?

Finger-Pointing and Void-Filling

Philosophers have asked this question for years, and the answer seems to lie buried in that extraordinary connection between the flaw and the self. It is a connection that we, as flawed people, cannot seem to separate. At times, we don't even want to, because, over time, the flaw becomes so much a part of our "self" that we fear letting it die. Without our familiar flaws, who would we be? Our totality would no longer be total. We would be incomplete, and worst of all, unfamiliar to our own, intimate selves. What would be left but a big, gaping, frightening void of potential? Yikes!

That, I believe, is where God steps in—in two ways. First, most people (myself most definitely included) cannot separate the good from the bad on our own. We can barely begin to identify all our flaws, much less separate ourselves from them. It's simply beyond our power to do so. And so we pray. I am sure that if we were to ask God to identify our faults, God would be more than happy to do so. But unlike ourselves, God forgives, so the risk is lower than if we do the finger-pointing ourselves. God acts as a kind of surrogate psychiatrist, probing those areas of our heart and soul where we cannot go alone.

Second, God helps to fill that frightening void. In general, people don't like voids. We don't like gaps in conversation, and we generally don't like a completely empty room. The most frightening thing in the universe, I think, is a black hole, which is like a void with an attitude—one that keeps sucking everything into it from light years around. But filling a void that was not only created *by* us, but is *of* us— since we have obviously invested a lot of ourselves in these "obstacles"—is really almost *beyond* us. The fact of the matter is that lasting spiritual and emotional change is generally beyond our capacity. We are too hesitant, or fearful; we regress, or move in the wrong direction. Instead, we must give ourselves over to something greater that can cushion the finger-pointing and ease the void-filling.

Logic in the Illogical

Then there is reality. A heavy dose of it is now right in front of me. I stare at the scrap of paper in my hands and try to point my finger at that single obstacle to faith. After some soul-searching, I know I've found the problem. The obstacle—again—is me. Great. Now I can get started. Except that removing the problem won't leave much room for faith-building.

In the previous chapter, the obstacle was tied to my past, just as we are all tied to that place. Connecting "then" with "now" helped to set the proper stage for "next." In this chapter, the issue of identity-as-obstacle lies more in how I, as well as my fellow agnostics and atheists, have been trained to think. First, we have been trained to resist just about anything that smacks of religion. We apply a cold, hard logic to seemingly squishy questions like faith. Added to this distrust of all things squishy, we tend to be skeptical of all institutions as well, particularly those that profess to have "the answer." No one is going to show us the way when we can get wonderfully lost by ourselves, thank you very much. In short, we like neither the message nor the medium of organized religion. And, to compound this problem, we tend to enjoy these traits. They are *our* faith. Logic and skepticism have served us well and kept us out of trouble—as well as out of a true faith, I suppose.

So let's turn again to that great religious cheat sheet, the Nicene Creed, and try to reconcile "faith" with faith. ***On the third day he rose again in fulfillment of the Scriptures; he ascended into heaven and is seated at the right hand of the Father.***

Naturally, I have thought a lot about this article of faith. For years, I would stand in church and recite only selected portions of the Creed. I accepted one God, and I believed Jesus suffered, died, and was buried—even doing this for our sake. I recited these phrases proudly. But when the ascension part rolled around, forget it. Too squishy. Over the years, however, I have come to believe that logic need not be sacrificed on this altar of religion. When it comes to *the* central question of Christianity, common sense does hold.

At the moment Christ died on the cross, his young movement was equally moribund. After several years of preaching to big crowds, his loyal followers could be counted on one hand. So destitute was this society that simply placing Jesus' defiled body in a tomb seemed like an act of courage compared to the complete rejection of almost everyone else. In short, without the kind of career make-over that would make Arnold Schwarzenneger proud, this new gospel according to Christ was heading exactly nowhere.

Yet, within a few days of his death the core group of believers had returned. In fact, they were so fired up, they spoke in defiance and in tongues to crowds who assumed they were drunk. Then they felt compelled to form churches throughout the known world. Not only that, they were willing to face vicious persecution and death for their efforts.

They must have been on to something, for the Church kept growing, and by the fourth century they had succeeded with their most politically important conversion of all—Constantine—who brought with him, as Emperor of Rome, a sizeable constituency.

From a purely logical point of view, *something* must have happened to turn this Christ-movement around. From a completely leaderless mush, Christianity became the most populous religion in the world. One can attribute the turnaround to an amazing public relations campaign, but it's hard to imagine a group of advertisers effectively duping whole armies of people into abandoning family, friends, and possessions for no obvious material or personal gain. It's hard to imagine a bunch of crazed PR executives convincing their customers to literally die for a product that offers some vague promise of salvation only after the customer has died. The early apostles must have been marketing geniuses. If only P.T. Barnum could have done so well, there would be a circus tent in every town!

Or maybe there really *was* a secret sauce. Maybe something extraordinary happened three days after Jesus was left for dead in a cave.

Like A Hanging in the Morning

As a Californian living in perpetual summer, I never appreciated death until I lived through several years on the East Coast. During each summer's worth of wild growth in a humid climate, the East Coast would be practically overrun with plant-life and raging insects. Everything seemed to sweat. Cicadas pounded through the night, and flies and mosquitoes kept us company by day, so that by the end of September I was almost begging for a good winter to kill off the excess. Without a good long chill, we would literally have been smothered with life.

In our culture, we fear and loathe death. Lent reminds us of its importance to life, and to faith. Christ's death was necessary not only for the Resurrection that followed, but for his followers as well. The crucifixion was a kind of sudden forced winter after the long summer of his ministry. The disciples had become perhaps too complacent with his miracles, the surety that he would always be present to calm the seas or to feed the crowds. As my father has said on more than one occasion, there is nothing like a hanging in the morning to focus the mind.

Death commands our attention like nothing else. Christ's death certainly helped to focus his followers. The crucifixion stripped away the cocoon that his earthly presence provided, and it gave a focal point for his movement into the future.

Lent gives us a glimpse of this reality. As Karen suggests, to die a little helps to strip away our own cocoon, keep focused, and prepare for our spiritual resurrection. I know *I've* done a lot of dying lately. With my old ways and assumptions suddenly out the door, I barely recognize "me" anymore. And that, I think, is precisely the point.

Christ's message is to break the mirror we've been gaping at so that we can fix the engine that drives our lives. What God helps us to do is to identify the obstacles to our own repair, to shed those obstacles, and then to fill the void with divine grace and presence. Christ leads by example. Having removed the only obstacle to everlasting life—his own death—he was able to ascend to God's grace. Having lived without sin, Christ had a certain advantage over the rest of us. But his final message is that spiritual ascension is possible for the lowliest of people. We just have to work a bit harder.

I take the pen and write "Me" on a piece of paper. Then, along with the others in our group, I lift a white votive candle from a broad bowl of water. The candle is lit. One by one, we put the paper to the flame and drop the charred paper onto the water. The ashes of our obstacles fizzle on the surface, and for a moment anyway, we do feel more complete.

CHAPTER 11

Being Judged

*He will come again in glory to judge
the living and the dead,
and his kingdom will have no end.*

With apologies to Neil Young: tonight's the rite, yes it is. After all this rambling on about good and evil, life and death, the time has come to put pen to paper—and not just a piece of scrap paper either. Tonight is the night for all the willing candidates and catechumens from our group to place our signature before God in the Book of the Elect. Once written, and blessed by our bishop two days later at a special ceremony, I become one of the elect, the chosen few. The signing is a public commitment to God and Church. After this, there really is no turning back—unless one wants to cancel all those wedding invitations (which one never does). That's why I've always considered this step three in my four-step journey to Christianity: as important as joining the RCIA, almost as significant as the final celebration. In my heart, I know it will be a celebration, a fantastic homecoming, if you will, for the prodigal son. But first I have to sign.

A Goat and a Promise

I lived for a year in West Africa and had the strange fortune to work at an old, refurbished textile factory. The factory made colorful print cloth for sale in local markets, and plain white underwear to sell to America. After six months of hard labor and a couple million dollars in investment, the factory was in debt and the underwear was not selling. So the local chieftains were brought in to sacrifice a goat on the factory grounds. The poor beast was led into a courtyard where, with remarkable gentleness, its throat was slit and the blood poured over the ground.

Needless to say, the sacrifice didn't change a thing. The company limped along for a few more years before closing down. Still, the ceremony was dramatic, and everyone seemed to have a good time for a while, dancing and singing of better days to come.

For some reason, I keep thinking of the Book of the Elect as our modern, sanitized version of a sacrificial ceremony. We don't have a lamb to slaughter. But we do have our signatures, which are a lot less messy on the church carpet.

Our signature is one of the few individual gestures we have left. In an age of instant copying, animal cloning, and anonymous computerized bytes whirring about the globe, it is astounding that we still require this ancient practice—the placement of one's mark on parchment made from actual trees—to make a document official. Saying "I do" before witnesses at a wedding is important, but it's hollow without that signature which is provided very privately, almost as an afterthought, after the "real" ceremony.

At some point in our lives, every one of us has

"practiced" our signature, in order to make it our own. I remember sometime in my teens, when I began signing for bank accounts and credit cards, I "tried on" several styles. There was the big decision about whether to write the S at the beginning of my name in cursive or in print. I thought the print version, followed by cursive for the rest of the name, looked the coolest, but I kept reverting to cursive for the whole name (the victim of third grade training) and had to give in to the inevitable. Clearly, I was not cool. Eventually, by default, I arrived at a slashing, almost illegible signature that has remained with me to this day.

Handwriting experts will testify that a signature is a window to our soul. A highly vertical slant in a person's script can indicate rigidity; full loops can suggest sexual drive. On the assumption that God is *the* expert—a religious forgery specialist—means God is going to have a ringside seat into my soul at the signing ceremony. God will review my quavering signature and see doubt, examine the incomplete letters and recognize fear. And God's judgment, as they say, will have no end. In short, no one should sign the Book of the Elect unless he or she is ready to Commit, with a capital C, because no one wants to be on the wrong side of that judgment. It is a place to be avoided.

Hell

In a charming novel, Garrison Keillor writes of a small congregation called the Sanctified Brethren. They are convinced that at any moment, without warning, Christ will sweep down in his Second Coming. If you were bad or found wanting on that particular day, well, that was just too bad for you. You and the other sinners would be left behind on Judgment Day, while the true believers, the good people of the earth who never had bad days, rose to glory. Even the Nicene Creed seems to agree. *He will come again in glory to judge the living and the dead, and his kingdom will have no end.*

What is most disconcerting, according to this statement, is that not only does God judge, God keeps permanent records. Makes our high school files seem truly harmless. According to the Creed, God's records last for eternity, and accompany the dead wherever they go. Otherwise, how would the Lord know who is on the roll call and who is not? Which begs the further question: Where do the living and the dead go when they are *not* invited into God's kingdom? The answer is obvious to those in the Sanctified Brethren. They are going to hell.

Soon after the landmark epistle to my parents, I had a long talk with my father about religion. One thing he said, for which I had no answer, concerned God's judgment. Essentially, my father's attitude is based on the Groucho Marx position concerning club membership. The great comedian with the painted moustache and the big cigar stated quite plainly that he would not want to join any club that would have him as a member. My father, however, takes a reverse twist concerning that big club in the sky called heaven. In short, he cannot believe in a God that would *not* allow him—a loving family man, a caring doctor, a non-Christian—into heaven.

For some Christians, the answer to my father's fate is clear. For me, it's not.

But before we get into the question of who's in and who's out, let's define the geography of these two paths. If heaven is a place where nothing ever happens, then hell is a literal hotbed of activity. We may think of hell as full of fiery demons, where there is a great deal of wailing and gnashing of teeth—in other words, a place you wouldn't want to take your sister even if she was being a pest. My favorite definition comes from our pastor—the same one who brought us the jugs in heaven. His opinion is that if hell does exist, it is likely no more nor less than the realization that one's soul will be denied God's love for eternity. The real wailing and gnashing comes from the knowledge that, having our once-in-a-lifetime opportunity to find God during our life, we refused that chance forever.

Thy Will

Having come from a strong base of non-believers, I have a pretty good understanding of what keeps agnostics from donning the label of Christian, even at the supposed risk of hell. One obvious reason is an inability to accept that God became human and that Jesus is one and the same. Fair enough, since the whole idea is admittedly far-fetched. But there is another reason, and it has little to do with belief. It is associated with the label itself.

For those outside the Church, those on the inside are viewed not so much as *righteous*, but as *self-righteous*. Having sat inside a church for a decade, I am happy to report that most Christians are not this way. They're just regular folks, with regular problems, and regular doubts about a host of issues. More important, priests are also human. They understand religious doubt, whether or not they share it. Their discernment processes are as thoughtful and difficult as anyone else's. Still, there is the public perception that Christians can be cruelly rigid concerning who's right and who's wrong and, *ipso facto*, who's going to hell and who isn't. I have often thought that if evangelizers of all denominations would present their faith as a journey, rather than an end point with a warning label, they would be far more successful in helping people along that journey.

The Catholic position is actually rather broad-minded on this score. In short, Catholics do not claim to know God's judgment. While the Church does believe that God's judgment upon our death is swift and immediate, *we* cannot know what that judgment will be. It is a level of doubt that we must live with and that can only be soothed by faith.

Tonight, as we collectively prepare to make our contract with this Church, all these issues of judgment and consequences are coming to a head. God does know our true heart, more surely than we know it, and will certainly pass judgment on whether our offering—be it goat or signature or firstborn son—is sincere. The question, at this point, is the sincerity of my commitment.

The Parking Lot

Meri and I drive to the church for the signing of the Book of the Elect. She is crying. If this faith journey has been hard on me, it has been doubly so for her. While her husband struggles before the gates of faith, she has remained supportive and stoic. As a lifelong Catholic, she has naturally and silently longed for the day when we could share that faith in our marriage. When we were first dating, I know she sighed briefly, but deeply, when I told her matter-of-factly about my "faith." I can still see the expression on her face. Not a deal-breaker, thank God, but not what she'd imagined either. For over ten years, through dating, engagement and marriage, life in Africa and on either side of the U.S., two children, and nine different jobs between us, she never pushed farther than I could go. Now, as I sit in the church parking lot on the edge of conversion, I balk. I say that I'm not ready. I don't think I can go through with it.

"Then don't," she says. She is not angry, only exasperated. And then the tears come. She says that no one is forcing me: not her; not God. She says the RCIA program repeats every year, and I can always go through this again if I'm not ready. That, of course, is both true and untenable. I don't think I could go through this again, and I don't think I'd be any further along if I did.

So what is it, then, that makes me hesitate? In seven short months, I have learned to see God and to pray. I have appreciated the Church's position on creation and on evil. I have even accepted the mystery in the virgin birth and found logic in the Resurrection of Jesus. In short, I have met every tenet so far in the Nicene Creed and learned to embrace them as my own. But, for some reason, it's not good enough.

We idle in the parking lot for a moment more, and then I switch off the motor. Meri asks if I would like to pray. I can think of nothing better. In the evening light, with my head bowed over the steering wheel, I ask God for a little help. Now would be a good time, since the ceremony is in fifteen minutes.

Strangely, I picture a vase in my mind. Maybe it's one of those heavenly jugs. The problem is that the vase is full of cracks, and I can tell, just by looking at it, that it won't hold water. My first instinct is to smooth out the cracks and make the surface perfect.

The image, of course, is my faith life. It's not perfect, so I'm certain that it won't hold under pressure. I am a little surprised that the symbol appears so easily, as if God had simply been waiting all this time for me to commission the painting. I open my eyes to the car dashboard and think I understand.

Meri reaches for my hand. "We should go in," she says.

CHAPTER 12

Free Will and the Flood of Faith

We believe in the Holy Spirit,
the Lord, the giver of life,
who proceeds from the Father and the Son.
With the Father and the Son he is
worshiped and glorified.
He has spoken through the Prophets.

My emotions in the parking lot were so familiar. I felt the same doubts on the threshold of fatherhood, because I had not yet memorized the child-rearing manual. The doubts have come again for conversion. I still can't, for example, recite the Creed with any confidence. But there is a clear difference between parenthood and faith. When Meri found herself with child, our proverbial train to parenthood had already left the station. There was no turning back and we simply got to enjoy *and* endure the ride until our miracle joined us in the world. With conversion, however, there is this funny thing called "free will."

The significance of free will is one of the fundamental

differences between Catholic and certain Protestant teachings. The subject is extraordinarily complex, but I'll give it a shot in a single paragraph. Protestant leaders like Martin Luther and John Calvin believed that salvation and sin came almost entirely from external sources—God and Satan, respectively. Faith alone saves us, and there is no requirement for our own self-motivated good works to get us into heaven. Calvin went so far as to teach that our lives are predetermined by God and that, in essence, we have no free will. But he was an extreme case. Catholic theologians put the onus, so to speak, on us. Sin is the result of our choice—a voluntary act—and not the call of the devil. Faith, likewise, is our choice—which is why hell is as much a mental state as it is a place, and it's compounded by the knowledge that we chose to reject God's grace. The message is that on this train called faith, I hold the brake. Not only that, but according to the Church, God gave me the brake, and I am more than free to use it.

In that parking lot, I was sorely tempted. I kept picturing the cracked vase, with the water seeping out. My faith seemed full of cracks. It couldn't hold anything, much less the Holy Spirit. The more I tried to smooth things over, the more water appeared around my fingertips. To make matters worse, the cracks were widening. The water pressure rose from inside the container. I could see that this game of spiritual Dutch boy at the dyke, trying to hold the dam together, was futile.

Clearly, the vase was not the issue here. It was the water inside. And as I could not stop it, there was nothing left to do but accept the flood.

Family

We enter the vestibule of the church and everyone who is in this RCIA story is there. The volunteer facilitators, who have been wonderfully supportive all these months, wait to greet us. They have guided our discussions and answered our questions all year. More important, they never conveyed a desire to "save our souls." They were more like spiritual real estate agents, without commission, who simply wanted to show us around the community. For that we are grateful.

There are our sponsors, who have served as confidantes and friends during the journey. The greatest contribution Doug has given to me is his assurance. I met him for breakfast on three separate occasions. Each time, I was certain that I had found some snag in my beliefs, some fine print in the Creed, that would be a show-stopper. Each time, as with our discussion of creation, he said I was ready.

Many of us have brought loved ones with us: a spouse, an uncle, a boyfriend. Two people are engaged to Catholics and their fiancés are here. We've become an extended family of sorts, sharing doubts and fears about faith that most people don't tell their closest friends.

Our parish employs four priests, which is incredible when you realize that many churches around the world have none and must rely on missionary priests to celebrate Eucharist. One thing I learned in school was, if you have a question, ask. I could fill a chapter with e-mail correspondence and meetings notes with our pastor and the other priests. I got to know them as people, and their honesty has been critical to my sense of trust in this large and at times unwieldy institution.

And there is Karen, who clearly loves her work. She's considered a bit of a renegade by some in our church. Her guitar-playing and candle-lighting are clearly rooted in the Baby Boomer generation, but it works, at least for me. She holds all these fractured souls together.

It is quite a group, and I know that I am going to miss this time when it passes. For all the difficulty, our time together has been refreshingly significant. In the daily grind, we rarely ask the big questions in life. That's the honest reason I attended church for so many years. Even though I sat in back and folded my arms before Communion, it was the only place where I ever heard anyone discuss the meaning of life, or how to live it well. RCIA is all this in overdrive. I'll remember this time forever.

Yet, to be honest, the evening's event is a blur. We had a potluck dinner that I barely remember. I spoke in a dream-state, I think, with Doug and Karen and many others. I know that Meri took Doug's wife aside and confided the turmoil of the last few months, and I remember her tears welling up again. But I was remarkably calm. Something had happened in the car that is hard to explain.

Holy Waters

As I tried to smooth the cracks in the vase, I kept thinking about what drew me to this religion in the first place, what sustained me through all those church gatherings as a non-believer. It was an attraction to the Holy Spirit.

Generations of scholars have tried to define the Holy Spirit. The Nicene Creed uses three sentences to make things clear. *We believe in the Holy Spirit, the Lord, the giver of life, who proceeds from the Father and the Son. With the Father and the Son he is worshiped and glorified. He has spoken through the Prophets.* The Holy Spirit is the giver of life, equal to the Father and the Son, and communicates through the prophets—as well as others who are open to hearing. In other words, the Holy Spirit is everywhere, the source and substance of life, the eternal fluid, if you will, that binds all things together and allows God to speak through us, the prophets of earth. This fluid, this water of life can no more be stopped than a rising tide.

As the water kept coming from the vase, despite my best intentions, I realized that what I was doing was impossible. If water is the giver of life, then I was trying to dam something that cannot be dammed. The Holy Spirit cannot be contained in a vessel. In fact, if the vase was somehow perfect, it would only serve as an obstacle to a naturally flowing faith.

My obsession with finding some perfectly smooth, rational, logical, and easily explainable belief system was, in truth, a Holy Grail. Such a thing does not exist. In seeing this Grail as nothing more than a cracked piece of pottery, I was able to let the Holy Spirit flow over me.

Hole-y Quilt

There is a lovely story of a group of women who were asked by Saint Peter to create a series of quilts as their gift for God upon entering the pearly gates of heaven. The quilts were to be made of the fabric of their lives, the panels representing all those things that had blessed them and for which they were grateful to God.

Most of the women took a lifetime to make their quilts. They kept them safe from harm in locked crates, and when they presented them to Saint Peter for approval, they were immaculate. The stitching was first-rate, the colors bright, and the patterns exquisite.

One woman, however, was ashamed. She had lived a difficult life, and could afford neither the time nor the money to fashion a solid quilt. She had used her quilt as a blanket for her children, later as a shawl to warm her sickly parents, and finally for herself. When she passed away, the thing was a mess, full of holes and ragged at the edges. At the gates of heaven, the woman reluctantly held her quilt to the light of God, which shone through the holes and fell upon her face. Eventually, she understood. Each hole that had been ripped apart by life was an opportunity for God to enter. Every frayed edge provided an opening for God to mend the seams. Unlike the other women, with their perfect quilts, this woman was bathed in divine Light.

The story is admittedly saccharine, but on this night, it became mine, although my story is of a cracked vase. The light of God is the unrelenting waters of the Holy Spirit. For others, it may be a different image: a perfectly sanded and varnished table where no spilled milk can penetrate the grain; or a closed harbor in which the holy sea (pun regretfully intended) is walled off from entering port.

Whatever the picture, the message is the same: God does not want perfect vessels. God does not want Tupperware™, hermitically sealed with the air burped out. God wants people, with all their cracks apparent, so the light…or the water…or the spilled milk can enter.

The Book

I leave the vestibule and the potluck dinner, and enter the chapel where the signing ceremony will take place. I feel, quite literally, as though I am floating—perhaps on water. Karen places us in a circle, with our loved ones and our sponsors at our sides. One by one, she asks our sponsors "the question": Are we, as Candidates and Catechumens, ready to assume the rights and responsibilities of full membership in the Catholic Community?

I fully expect Doug to say no, not yet. He may say I am a good guy, even with good intentions, but as David said, the road to hell is paved with them. But Doug declares that I am definitely ready. I keep expecting a bolt from heaven to strike us both. I close my eyes and wait for hell to open, but nothing. Maybe God just doesn't want to damage the sanctuary.

Then Doug does an amazing thing: he praises the doubts, and my incessant questions poured out over syrupy waffles. He says we come to a mature, adult faith only by searching for it. Then he places his hands on my shoulders and says he is confident that I have found God through Christ, and that I will love them both with heart, soul, and mind.

Karen holds out the pen, and I step forward to take it. I move to the center of the circle and write my name in the Book of the Elect. This is the big leap forward. This is my offering to God, my binding commitment. I give my signature over—and feel a great weight lifting from my shoulders. Never in my entire life have I made such a major step with less certainty *and* less anxiety—which is to say that I have embraced the unknown and the unknowable, and let the cleansing waters of the Holy Spirit wash away all fears. If God can accomplish *this* miracle of the soul, who am I to doubt God's powers of transformation? To twist Groucho Marx around again, I am ready to join a community that will accept me.

I return the pen to Karen and walk straight to Meri. We embrace. With a gesture of the hands and the calm in my eyes, I assure her that I finally know what I am doing, and more important, that it is the right thing to do. She seems to understand, for now. (There will be hours of discussion later.) After everyone has signed the book, Karen lights a candle and the flame is passed from one to another until over thirty lit candles encircle the room.

The Bishop

The next day, on a Sunday in March, we drive to another church in a neighboring city. We are to meet the bishop at a special service for the newly elect. Hundreds of people from all over the diocese are present. They have come to join the community.

It is a beautiful ceremony. The bishop walks slowly down the aisle, with his crozier (fish-hook staff) in hand and the tall mitre (hat) resting somewhat precariously on his head. He is followed by a coterie of altar servers and assistants, and I am reminded of the pomp and circumstance that this church conveys so well. It is a celebration two thousand years in the making. The bishop encourages and blesses us, and we feel both in abundance. We even get a couple of photos with him after the service.

On the drive home, I mention to Meri how so much of this journey has seemed beyond my control. Try as I might to nail the Spirit down, to find flaws or loopholes, to impose a little logic, it pours out of my grasp until I am drenched by its waters. The surprising thing is not so much that I cannot contain the Spirit, or even that I have been doused by it, but that I actually had no hope of finding it on my own. The whole journey seems to have occurred without any free will on my part, as if the train brake was just a prop. Against my better judgment, I climbed down from the fence. Despite my best intentions, I signed up for the RCIA. Now I am poised on the threshold of Christianity. Clearly, somebody was driving this train, and it wasn't me.

I remember an exercise Karen presented to the group as we prepared for the coming of Lent. In typically cheerful fashion, she asked each of us to write our own epitaph. Mine came out of the blue, like that cracked vase in the car, and I entered it quickly into my faith journal. But now the words have a whole different meaning—as if they were written not for a gravestone, but for a birthstone on an Easter weekend.

My work is done; I'm all drawn in.
God found me. He lies herein.

CHAPTER 13

Who Are These Guys?

We believe in one holy catholic and apostolic Church.

For the past three Masses, I have watched the non-baptized in our group receive their exorcisms. This is not some head-spinning ordeal, but an integral part of the Scrutinies. During the Scrutinies, those of the elect who have never been baptized walk up to the front of our church and kneel before the congregation. In some churches, they lie prostrate before the altar. In the early Church, they would kneel on an animal skin, to symbolize the rejection of their basic nature. Our church does neither, which has been just fine with us, for the real power of the ceremony is in the words themselves. With their sponsors standing behind, hands on the elect's shoulder, the priest calls for all inner darkness to be lifted and all hearts to be filled with the Holy Spirit. The priest then lays hands on each of the elect and bids them to rise in preparation for their baptism on Easter.

Since I was baptized long ago, I do not participate in this ceremony. Nevertheless, it is powerful. When we leave before the serving of the Eucharist, there is a holy cleanliness in the air around us, as if we had experienced a great purging of the soul.

When we enter the vestibule, we are greeted by fan mail. All in all, it is quite heady stuff. I get letters now, every week. A poster board has been hung in the vestibule with photos of every one of the elect. Below the photos are our names, and below these are paper pockets for an ever-increasing number of letters and notes of encouragement. I get them now from friends, as well as strangers. In one letter, a woman recalls her own conversion and says it was one of the best experiences of her life. In another, a member of the Knights of Columbus asks me to call him after Easter; he's holding a fund-raiser and needs help. It is the collective opening of this community: the *one holy catholic and apostolic Church.*

With all this fanfare, it is easy to get caught up in the excitement. It's like coming into port on a great ocean liner with a crowd full of dignitaries waiting at the dock. But, great skeptic that I am, one question still remains.

After nine months of soul searching, I have come to know God, Jesus, and the Holy Spirit bit by bit. But those dignitaries on the dock, and the institution that houses them, remain a mystery. Once again, unfortunately, the question is critical to conversion, for it is the institution rather than the faith, I think, that drove my parents away.

First Things First

At the outset, it's important to clear up a misconception shared by almost every non-Catholic, including me: the word "catholic" in the Nicene Creed is written with a small c.

When I first attended church, I thought the word began with a big C. I thought the Catholics were effectively saying, "We believe in us!"—sort of like a collective "Go Team!" near the end of the Creed. I have since learned that the meaning is entirely different.

For those who like definitions, I refer to what is probably the most used dictionary in the modern world: that pull-down Thesaurus in your word processing toolbar. Here, "catholic" has the following synonyms: wide-ranging, all-embracing, and varied. Interestingly, a single antonym is suggested: conservative. Of course, Catholic leaders have their own take on the word: They speak of a "universal church," one that is far-reaching, all-encompassing, and grounded in timeless truth.

The word finds its first official endorsement in the Apostles' Creed. Once again, this was partly directed at those heretical Gnostics who believed that true enlightenment came only through true understanding of Christ's teachings. They also believed that the most important Christian doctrines, which formed the basis for true understanding, should be reserved for a select few. In other words, they were a lot like certain bank tellers who say you can't open an account unless you complete a certain form, but you can't access the form unless you have an account with a minimum balance. The early Church leaders, in contrast, wanted anyone to be able to open an account in the ever-expanding Bank of God. Thus the word "catholic" was installed, so to speak, into their mission statement. At its core, this was to be a Church that was inclusive, just as Christ himself was inclusive of so many us who might be considered risky accounts—sort of like universal checking on a timeless deposit.

The word "apostolic" yields nothing in the word processing universe. In more conventional dictionaries, "apostolic" means something that is born out of the apostles' teachings, referring of course to the first apostles of Jesus—the original eleven, excluding Judas Iscariot, plus Matthias, who was added in a kind of straw vote. More important, the Church's position is that "apostolic" refers to the unbroken chain of Christ's word that was passed directly from Jesus to Peter, the "Rock" of the Church and first pope; and then from generation to generation, down through the centuries to the present.

But "apostle," like almost every word, also has a broader meaning, e.g., follower, or messenger, or disciple. In that context, every member of the Church is apostolic. Everyone is a follower; everyone is a messenger; everyone is a disciple. It is an organic structure that, at least in theory, is wonderfully self-perpetuating.

And what of "holy"? The word comes first in the list of three, and serves to define them. If anything, the Church *is* and *wants to be* holy—sacred, blessed, and consecrated by the Holy Spirit. It seeks to promote the holy word of God on earth, and that, to coin a phrase, is a beautiful thing. In all the divisiveness that surrounds this grand institution, sometimes the centrality of this intent, this message, is lost. Fundamentally, the Church is made up of people who are dedicated to, and searching for, the love of God.

Together, this grouping of terms not only defines the Church, it also directs the institution in what it would like to be: sacred, universal, born, and reborn of the teachings and traditions of Jesus and the apostles. By reciting this line of the Creed, we are entering into that mission.

Saints Alive

Still, this definition of "church" is not what kept people like me and my parents away. Indeed, the seeds of separation can be found in two items not even mentioned in the Nicene Creed. So while the Creed has definitely lit my journey to Catholicism, I figure it's a good time to turn up the high beams, however briefly, on a few potential bumps in the road.

First, we have the saints. In short, my family never understood this passion for heavenly ghosts. Truth be told, we laughed, and figured it was evidence that Catholics were a bit soft in the head. The communion of saints (which *is* cited in the Apostles' Creed) seemed like little more than a series of pictures, trinkets, and dashboard statuettes that people pray to in order to get that coveted parking space or a winning lottery ticket. In other words, it seemed silly, even idolatrous.

I remember laughing snidely at my Irish Catholic grandmother who told me to give a Saint Christopher medal to a girl to show my adolescent love; and at my neighbor who advised us to bury a statue of Saint Joseph upside down in the backyard when we wanted to sell our house. And the sheer numbers of saints seemed to border on absurdity— more than twenty-five hundred of them! There is a saint for accountants, tax collectors, and security guards (Matthew), and two saints who can be called upon to prevent twitching (Bartholomew, who was flayed alive, and Bishop Cornelius). There are famous saints like Augustine, who truly defined the Church, and there are others who are downright obscure, like Eustace, who may have been either a Syrian priest or an Egyptian martyr. In 1969, the Roman Catholic Church dropped a number of saints from the liturgical calendar because of doubts that they had ever actually lived. (Among these was Christopher, which put a big dent in the middle-school dating scene.) So I can be forgiven, perhaps by Jude, the patron of lost causes, or by Teresa of Avila, who helps people in serious need of grace. In truth, I never realized the significance of this communion until my Inquiry days, when we were encouraged to ask pointed questions about the Church. I learned that in the Roman Catholic Church, saints are people who were martyred or led a particularly holy life, had miracles associated with them in life or after death, and have a special place in Catholic culture. If that person lived after A.D. 1000, the Church has a rigorous process, canonization, that determines whether this person will be added to the official list of saints. If the person was born more than a millennium ago, he or she gets a break: the saintly title may be used according to custom.

Mary the Mother of Jesus is the primary saint. Angels are also considered saints. And in traditional belief, all Christians on earth and all the saints in heaven are considered members of the holy, catholic, and apostolic Church.

It is this last distinction that is so important. Just as living members of the Church seek the prayers of each other, and even share in the good *and* bad deeds of each other, so the living can ask those in heaven for their prayers. This says a lot about the afterlife—a dominion of souls, wholly intact, who remain with us in spirit. But it says even more, I think, about the primacy of community in this great faith.

Friends of mine from other faiths speak with a kind of reverence about the Catholic strength in community. The

Catholic schools, hospitals, charities, youth groups, and associations that populate the world are a living testament to the Catholic penchant for community and good works. The communion of saints simply extends this community—all the way to heaven. In a sense, the Catholic community is not only extensive, it is eternal.

In fact, the communion of saints offers us a lesson we all could relearn: that the communion of people, alive and dead, is holy; that, as an eternal community, we should be able to turn to each other, on earth and in heaven, to find comfort, to pray, and to seek a neighbor or a saint to intercede on our behalf. And in that context, perhaps a dashboard saint is not so ridiculous after all. It's a bit like having a picture of your favorite aunt or uncle in the car, to keep you company on the road.

Even the great skeptic (me) found a saint for my faith journey. She is Saint Thérèse of Lisieux. Known as the Little Flower, she is often portrayed as the picture of innocent devotion. But David gave me the real scoop one day. She was feisty, stubborn, and even a trifle spoiled. The thing I appreciate is that she was normal, average, imperfect. During the last months of her life, as she was dying of tuberculosis at age 24, she had doubts about her faith, doubts about God. What she did was to offer her doubts up for others, so they would know they were not alone. She understood that, when one is doubting, it's nice to have company. And so she has been my consummate companion for this long trip. Maybe I should put her on my dashboard.

Herding Cats

The second item for my family was the position of the pope. In its 2,000-year history, the Catholic Church has had more than two-hundred-fifty popes, from Peter down to the present day. Some have been remarkable, others bland. Some presided over great flowerings in the Church, others over the Spanish and Roman Inquisitions. In that sense, their histories read like the leaders of any great institution, including the United States. But there is one issue concerning the papal position that, for most non-Catholics, seems to transcend all others: papal infallibility.

Actually, this is a relatively recent proclamation. In 1869, Pope Pius IX was literally under siege in Italy while the Roman Catholic Church was fraying at the edges. Huge tracts of land were taken from Church control, and religious authority was increasingly ignored. In an attempt to exercise some authority over a cabal of kings and revolutionaries, the pope gathered the First Vatican Council. The following year, he proclaimed the dogma of papal infallibility. There are limits on when this may be invoked, and since that time only one statement exercising the solemn magisterium has been made, concerning the "Assumption of the Virgin Mary into Heaven," by Pope Pius XII in 1950—through the dogma of the Immaculate Conception, issued in 1854, is often grouped with the proclamation. Nevertheless, the doctrine itself does seem to lend weight to every speech or encyclical, that comes from the papacy.

This book is clearly about faith, not doctrine. Yet an outsider, I could never separate the two; my parents still can't. So it's not unreasonable to pause before this threshold of

Church to survey this realm of the land. The Church would not, itself, separate the two, as it continues to place great emphasis on both teachings *and* tradition—which are frequently ratified and codified as doctrine by the pope. Throughout its history, leaders of the Catholic hierarchy have struggled in this regard—to get their "followers" to, for want of a better term, follow. I imagine it is a bit like herding cats. The Nicene Creed is just one example of a successful herding program.

But what a lot of cats: over nine-hundred-million Catholics at last count, with more every year. That is well over three times the population of the U.S., which has a single President, serious divisions over his proclamations, and universal adherence. My wife raised this analogy years ago, when I very rationally suggested she leave the Church because she disagreed with some edict from Rome. She calmly mentioned some recent legislation signed by the White House, then suggested we leave the U.S. and find a new country to join. Not fair, I argued; if we don't like our leaders, we can always vote for new ones. She could too, she said, through prayer; her "democratic process" was the Holy Spirit. Eventually, I realized her allegiance ran much deeper than the people at the top. It was, in fact, the people at the middle and at the bottom who kept her in this community. It was the people in her family.

Big C, little c

When I first began this journey, the Big C word was Catholic—an imposing word that spoke of empires and huge gothic cathedrals. Now I understand the power of the small c—the universal, inclusive, and catholic church; the significance of an eternal communion of saints; and the life-giving grace of a community in faith. These are powerful words, for they ground clergy, religious, and lay members of the Church in both the Holy Spirit and the community that keeps that Spirit alive. In the end, the power of the one, holy, catholic, apostolic church is realized in this community.

I believe, and have felt from the very beginning, that I would not have chosen the Catholic path on my own. There were simply too many obstacles in my past for me to head in this particular direction. By virtue of another holy institution, marriage, the path effectively chose me. Like the line from my Irish grandmother's favorite blessing, this road of faith did seem to literally rise up to meet me. My wife and children put me here. Their faith guided me in the direction of this larger faith family, and now that I stand at the gates of this great community, I can only say that, despite its factions and foibles, I am grateful. I never would have asked these painful questions of faith without their faith in me. I would never have had the strength to climb down from the fence without their support. What awaits on the other side of that Easter celebration, I can only guess at—but I am sure that it awaits with open arms.

The feeling is best captured in one of those letters, tucked anonymously in the poster board pocket beneath my photo in the vestibule. It is my favorite letter, and it is the shortest of them all. It reads: "Welcome to the family."

CHAPTER 14

Sacraments and Rituals

We acknowledge one baptism
for the forgiveness of sins.

My first experience with Eucharist was, to put it bluntly, an embarrassment. It happened at a church in the Boston area that had no separate blessing for people, like me, who would not receive Communion. As a result, during Eucharist I would sit quietly while Meri and the rest of the congregation filed past for the body and blood of Christ. I felt like an outsider, and this seemed kind of a shame, particularly after sharing an opening procession, several songs, three readings, and a homily with so many nice people.

One day, after a moving homily about a loving and inclusive God, I figured, what the heck. I would take them up on their unspoken invitation and join them in celebration as a bonding experience, an expression of solidarity with my fellow faith-seekers.

Without warning anyone, and while Meri was well ahead in the procession for the Eucharist, I stood. Surveying the church with affection, I waited reverently in line for the host.

When I faced the priest, he held up a small piece of bread, said "The body of Christ," and placed it in my hand. I didn't know what to say, so I responded as any polite person should when given a gift. I said, "Thank you."

The priest looked a little flustered, but I left before he could respond. I was pretty flustered myself, and forgot to take the wine. Still, I was proud of myself, and later I proudly told Meri of my accomplishment. To my distress, she was mighty distressed!

And so I was introduced to the true meaning of sacrament.

The first thing I learned was that Church sacraments are much more than empty rituals or nice bonding events for the faithful. They actually mean something! In a word, sacraments and rituals are the verbs, the action words of faith. Just as people need to move, to do, sacraments provide a vehicle to engage those around us, which is really the essence of church, of why we come together in the first place. Without the sacraments, the community itself would not have as much vibrancy, or even unity.

The second thing I have learned, over the course of many years, is that the sacraments have come to mean something to *me*. They offer a window onto the pomp and significance of this institution. Each sacrament, in its own way, has helped me to understand the purpose of church, and through them I have come to engage the community as well. Together, they serve as a siren song for faith.

Well before I ever considered conversion or RCIA, the beauty of such sacraments as matrimony and baptism offered a glimmer of the powerful and faith-filled side of the Catholic tradition. I had never appreciated this side before. The sacraments were a proclamation that here is a community of substance, here is a people of faith; herein lies God.

For this insight alone, they are worth exploring, particularly since my earlier attempt at sacrament was not so promising.

Wedding Song

My first conscious experience with a sacrament came late in life: at my wedding. In retrospect, the journey to the altar mirrors my journey to faith, for initially the bride-to-be and I had little in common. That cold realization came early in our courtship. I was talking with Meri in my dorm room at graduate school when she noticed a set of guitar songbooks on the shelf. "So," she said, "I see you like Bob Die-lan."

When I answered, I am sure I managed a straight face—she was a lovely woman and not to be trifled with—but inside I thought, "Oh, no, this will never work."

Something, however, obviously compelled me onward. I cut my hair shorter, stopped wearing beads, went to church, and followed her to Africa for a year. My parents were happy as well, particularly about the hair and beads. And when we returned from Africa, we were married. A priest who was a friend of Meri's family witnessed the ceremony, called the sacrament of matrimony. Together, we joined in those beautiful rituals of wedding—the unity candle to bind our two families; the vows of marriage; the exchange of rings—all steeped in the richness of the Church. Surrounded by friends and family, we sang the theme song from a tough year in Africa, *Be Not Afraid*.

At my side, Meri's voice was as full and radiant as I had ever heard. And when the priest "presented" us to the community, everyone applauded.

The wedding was beautiful, but it is the marriage that has paved the way for faith. Obviously, my road to Catholicism has been aided greatly by my Catholic wife, but it goes deeper than that. To this day, marriage and faith are joined at the hip, for it is the confidence I have found in the marriage that has bolstered my confidence for God. Marriage has allowed me to go beyond what I thought I knew about God and Church, just as I went beyond "Die-lan" in courtship, to find a deeper value in faith. Without the one, I doubt that I could have pursued the other.

One Baptism, Two Families

My next glimpse of the sacraments came through the sacrament of baptism. In Dahlgren Chapel at Georgetown University, near where we lived for several years, we witnessed the best baptisms ever. The babies were often cute, and they always looked stunned when they were dipped three times into a bowl of holy water. But it was a young and jovial priest who made the difference. When he held the baby out to the congregation and welcomed the new member of the Catholic family, he was radiant. Everyone applauded, as much for his smile, I think, as for the child. Through this sacrament, and this man, I realized for the first time that maybe, just maybe, there really was something to this faith, for where else could such joy come from?

A few years later, our son and daughter were baptized, and that changed everything. Now it was no longer Meri as

Catholic and me as, well, not. Now we were bound together, as family, in this strange institution. I could no longer separate myself, nor did I want to. Again, it was the sacrament that opened my eyes to what I had been missing, this time in two ways.

First, baptism is a tangible sense of continuity between God and the people God has fashioned. The biblical symbol for birth is water. In the earliest moments of creation, Genesis tells us how the Spirit of God hovered over the waters, and how God separated water from water. We are thus born of the water. It seems only right that we should be baptized by it as well. When our own two children were held aloft, dripping wet from the baptismal font, I felt as if I was witness to the birth of two new worlds. Surely, even God could not have been more pleased. The priest who held our children was the same one who had witnessed our sacrament of matrimony, which served to bring this continuity home—from God's great creation to mine, through marriage. It is a continuum to the very Source of time, and baptism grounds this timelessness in the day-to-day of family.

The second eye-opener brought my faith home in a more literal way. Of all the meanings to baptism—that it is necessary for the remission of sins and for the infusion of grace—I have been most touched by the sense that, through baptism, we all become adopted children of God. All those who have been baptized are, thus, of two families—including me. As our still damp children were placed into my arms, and the priest sealed them with the Holy Spirit through the sign of the holy oil of chrism, I recognized this fact. I could literally see myself in the same position long ago, when it had been my turn to be baptized. In the instant of seeing my own children transformed by water and oil, I realized that I too had been adopted long ago. That these two families, led by my parents on one side and the Church on the other, are not on speaking terms is not unusual. But once again, the power of this sacrament changes everything. It means that this RCIA program is no longer a journey to the unknown. It's more like a family reunion, a good way to get to know some long lost relatives.

No wonder this journey has felt, at times, like coming home.

Healing Sacraments and the Tenderloin Touch

Two other sacraments are known collectively as the sacraments of healing. In their capacity to touch and to heal our frail humanity in precisely those places where we are the most vulnerable, these sacraments are enough to make a grown agnostic weep. To me, they are the calling cards of faith, for they are compelling and available to all.

The first is called the sacrament of penance and reconciliation, otherwise known as "confession." My first reconciliation occurred recently, during Lent. As preparation for Easter and our first Catholic Eucharist, Karen asked us to arrange confession with a priest of our choosing. I am not particularly sinful, but I was mighty nervous. I kept thinking of old movies and new TV shows where some poor blighter, racked by guilt, enters a dark confessional, kneels down, and slides open a screened panel door. Behind the screen, a mysterious priest hears the sins recited with a cringe of remorse, and then dutifully exacts penance before God.

Naturally, I chose the kindest and gentlest priest I knew, a wonderful man from the Philippines named Father Geoff. In the end, the experience was a gift.

I entered a simple room in the rectory of our church, and sat in a lightly upholstered chair. Father Geoff sat opposite and pulled his chair so close that our knees almost touched. In our daily lives, we never sit this way; we either face in different directions or have something between us, like a solid table. It was at once disconcerting and intimate. Immediately, I forgot the prayer we were told to recite for first reconciliation: *Oh my God, I am sorry for my sins....* The lines simply vanished, and I was certain of failure: no reconciliation this time.

I am relieved to say that Hollywood has it wrong. Not only has face-to-face penance largely replaced the old confessional booth, but Vatican II has fostered other changes as well. Nowadays, priests focus more on the healing power of God than a recitation of fifteen Hail Mary's for penance. A weekly confession is also no longer the norm for receiving Eucharist at Sunday Mass. But priests and the Church take the sacrament no less seriously. A priest is bound by God not to reveal one's confession to anyone, even at the risk of jail time or worse. And the penance that is issued is still designed for the most important reason imaginable, to serve as a reminder of God's gift of forgiveness and as a touchstone for the restoration of his grace.

Despite such changes, I blurted out what every movie-scripted confessee has said for decades: "Forgive me, Father, for I have sinned." Apparently, Father Geoff has watched the same movies, because he accepted the attempt. Within minutes, the priest and I were chatting away about my various transgressions. He gave no traditional guilt lashings—but did call for a change of attitude, which is just what I needed at the time—and then he placed his hands on my head and blessed me.

To be touched in blessing, with the intent of healing, is also rare. We are so inundated with TV touch, Madison Avenue Touch, selling sex to get-you-to-buy touch, that we have forgotten the touch of grace. Such touch-without-expectation is a gift without bounds. It can even be self-perpetuating, just as love is.

In the Tenderloin, a rundown section of San Francisco, this gift is perpetuated freely. There, a church community sends its members on a ministry of touch. They wade into the mean streets of the city to find the poor and the miserable. Then, without fuss, the ministers kneel down and make contact—with the touch of a hand, a non-hostile voice, occasionally some food—to make the homeless feel a little more human. Sometimes I think the countless poor souls among us could all use this: something to make us feel more human. With Father Geoff's hands on my head, and his words of reconciliation in the air, I felt the beauty of a heavenly touch. We all need such blessings, if for nothing more than to remember our humanity and to know that the door to grace is always open.

The second of these healing sacraments is also about touch. Formerly known as extreme unction and typically reserved for the dying, it is now called the anointing of the sick and is for all who are seriously ill. In our church, on one special day of the year, the priest makes a communal call. He asks those at Mass who are legitimately ill in body, mind, or spirit to come forward for a blessing. I am always shocked by the numbers, as over a third of the congregation walks down the aisle. The cross is traced with blessed oil on their hands and forehead, and then they return to their pews to pray.

As a hardened agnostic, I was quite humbled at this display of grace. There are more people in pain than we realize. To witness firsthand the power of spiritual healing, its ability to pull people from their pews and call them down the aisles, was further evidence that something of significance was at work here. It was as if I was witnessing a glimmer of God through those most intimately touched by the divine.

Holy Orders, Confirmation, and Jealousy

There are three other holy sacraments, out of a total of seven, that I have not yet experienced. The first, holy orders, I probably never will, although deacons can be married men. Called ordination, this sacrament is reserved for deacons, priests, and bishops—just as matrimony is reserved for married couples; and it is coupled with matrimony as a sacrament of service and communion. These two are often called the "social sacraments," as they are meant to convey the ideal of loving all God's people and bringing about the reign of God among us.

The second two, confirmation and Eucharist, are linked with baptism as a sacrament of initiation. When one is confirmed in the faith, he or she is sealed with the fullness of the fruit of the Holy Spirit. I will be experiencing both confirmation and Eucharist very soon.

To be honest, I have been somewhat jealous of my friends in the RCIA who will be baptized. After signing the Book of the Elect, the baptized-to-be have been singled out for special treatment. They now wear a full-length sackcloth over their clothes during Mass, a symbol of simplicity, and they are often mentioned by the priests during dismissal. More dramatically, they will wade into a large baptismal pool and be drenched with water at the Easter Vigil. Not that I long to wear sackcloth or be doused with water in a church, but I do find myself explaining to others that I am *only* going to be confirmed on Easter.

Thankfully, my new sense of baptism has washed away this jealousy. Confirmation is the conscious commitment—as opposed to, say, infant baptism—to the Catholic Church. Normally, the sacrament is reserved for seven- to seventeen-year-olds. It also perpetuates the grace of Pentecost in the Church.[5] But confirmation's greatest significance, for me, it what it is *not*: It is not a re-baptism. Catholic teaching makes perfectly clear that baptism is a once-and-forever sacrament. In other words, once is enough. In fact, of all the sacraments, the Nicene Creed mentions only this one. **We *acknowledge* one baptism for the forgiveness of sins.**

The rationale for this statement is simple and inspired. To put it succinctly, God's grace is sufficient and complete. We don't need periodic tune-ups or a holy oil change to keep the motor running. If anything, reconciliation serves as the tune-up, and anointing of the sick as a transfusion for the spirit. As for baptism, once the grace of God has descended upon us, we are blessed forever.

So, in the end, I am satisfied. Two families is quite enough for one person.

Eucharist—Completing the Circle, Heading Home

A true appreciation for Eucharist, the final and perhaps holiest of the seven sacraments, was actually forced upon me by Karen. She innocently suggested I create a simple ritual for our last official meeting of the RCIA. When she said the ritual should emphasize the sacredness of Eucharist, I almost choked. If only she knew of my first attempt.

Over the years, I have learned that Eucharist is the very heart and soul of the Church. As the *Catechism* proclaims, it is "the source and summit of the Christian life." In other words, it is not to be taken lightly (or received in a moment of good cheer to bond with one's neighbor down the pew). In short, Eucharist is not just a symbol. When the bread and wine are consecrated during Mass, they are transubstantiated (I finally got to use that word) into the body and blood of Christ. Other faiths find this hard to swallow, so to speak, which is why I have finally come to accept that the Church is right in limiting Eucharist to those who embrace its full meaning.

At the same time, I now have also come to accept that our narrow minds may simply not appreciate the enormity, or shape, or substance of Christ's heavenly body and blood. Because we do not understand this (or many other miracles) does not make it any less plausible. The meaning of Eucharist is thus the acceptance of the Real Presence of Christ into our hands and, along with a blessing, into our bodies. From my limited perspective, this is where the most surprising miracle occurs, at the moment of public transformation when we, as a people, receive the sacred host into our own earthly one. It is then we are joined into the body of Christ, into the community of God.

That said, all Karen wants from me is a simple ritual to capture the heart and soul of the Church; to ensure that it be meaningful and respectful; and to be no more than ten minutes long. In a Church where there is no such thing as a "simple" ritual, where every act is weighted in pomp and import and a whole lot of history, I wonder if this ritual is my penance for that little "mistake" with the Eucharist ten years ago.

Our final session begins smoothly enough. Karen reminds us of our group retreat in three days, and warns us that the pace of events then increases straight on to the Easter Vigil. She is concerned and earnest, and her excitement is contagious.

After a final breakout session, where we discuss the meaning of Eucharist and sing a last rendition of *This is Our Room*, Karen turns to me and nods. I ask the group to form a circle while Karen gives everyone a single, unconsecrated wafer—the kind that will become Eucharist during Mass. Holding this small token, that represents the culmination of so many long months of learning and sharing, is a poignant hint of things to come. We stare into our hands. Then the group is instructed to break the wafer into two pieces. This seems downright blasphemous, but Karen assures us that it isn't since the wafer is unconsecrated. With some reluctance, we break the unleavened bread, and then I make the first move.

Within our circle of friends, I turn to the right and give half of my wafer to David as I bless him. He places the bread in his mouth and swallows. After a brief silence, David takes the remaining half from my hand and gives it back to me with his blessing. Then he turns and gives half of his wafer to Amy, and the circle continues around until I complete the ritual with Karen, who is on my left.

The breaking of the wafer symbolizes the breaking of the bread, of course. When we feed and bless the others in the circle, and are fed and blessed by them, we feed and bless our community. When the group completes the circle, we make it whole.

We acknowledge the moment, and then reverently go our separate ways for the evening. In the end, a sacrament has been honored. And we have received a preview of something momentous, coming very soon to a church near us.

CHAPTER 15

Source and Summit

We look for the resurrection of the dead,
and the life of the world to come.

Out of the more than two hundred words about faith and hope and history and commitment, the Creed ends with a command: Look! *We look for the resurrection of the dead, and the life of the world to come.*

There is a broad meaning to this phrase. It is, in many respects, the summation of everything we learned this year: the need to die in Christ in order to be resurrected in his light; the promise of everlasting life in a Godly heaven. But it also, I think, reflects the underlying message of the RCIA, which is about deliverance *now*, in preparation for a new life *here*. In using these action words—to move, to do, to look—the Creed issues as its grand finale a call to act. God knocks, but we must actually open the door. God shines, but we have to see.

At the same time, there is an old saying that if you want to make God laugh you should tell him your plans. Well, I planned to be a lot of things, and a Catholic Christian was not one of them. If it were up to me, I never would have climbed onto that spiritual fence. I'd be on solid ground—unfulfilled, perhaps, but quite comfortable, thank you. Yet, here I am. God must be rolling in the aisles. Now for the punch line: I believe that I had little to do with it. How, after all, can you *decide* on a longing for God? How can you realistically *choose* faith?

As we reach the end of the RCIA, it is time to reconcile this holy dichotomy between nature—the seed of our longing—and nurture—epitomized in the Creed's call to act, to grow the seed. In other words, it's time to move from this preparation for faith to lifelong practice, from elect to Christian, from playing at Eucharist to the real thing.

Resurrection and the Life

Looking back, the year has been one long season of Advent and Lent, all rolled together. We have waited anxiously for a kind of rebirth, and we have been asked to die. While not as dramatic as the Book of Exodus, or even *Finding Nemo*, our journey has been epochal to us. Along the way, we have made ourselves vulnerable before God and before each other. I will miss it.

Our final gathering is at a retreat house in the hills. We gather with Karen and the other leaders to celebrate the end and the beginning, and to share our personal experiences of the past year. David relates the arguments he's had with his Protestant grandparents, who feared he would make them eat fish on Fridays. An older man, Franco, had to battle internal demons, including alcoholism, in order to find himself in the Church. Amy, making the difficult conversion from

Mormonism, has still not told her parents, and perhaps she never will. In everyone, there has been some act of bravery to get to here. Faith is never easy.

By evening, we are joined for a potluck supper by our significant others and our sponsors. It is time to says "thanks" for putting up with us this past year: absorbing our questions, doubts, and endless mood-swings; sacrificing the time we've spent away from home for weekly sessions. We offer toasts. Then we separate for an hour of silent reflection, to think about what we have done and what we are about to do.

We rejoin in a candle-lit room. Karen is playing the guitar. There is the familiar bowl of water, and the familiar candles floating on the surface. Karen tells us that we are to receive a blessing from our "saint" on earth. She circles the room with a porcelain dish of oil and stops before each pair of people.

When she reaches Meri, Karen asks her to dip a finger into the oil and trace the sign of the cross on my forehead. Meri blesses my longing and my search, and prays that they continue. She closes with an Irish blessing: "May the road rise to meet you. May the wind be always at your back. May God hold you closely in the palm of God's hand." I smile, and imagine God and my grandmother sharing a laugh.

Karen closes with a blessing of her own. She speaks of the journey we have taken together and the commitment we are about to make as a holy people, apostles of God, and members of the Catholic community. She tells of the Easter Vigil: the pageantry we will witness, the holiness of the sacraments in which we will participate.

It is a blessing of confidence. When we leave the hall, we are all pointed in the same direction.

Fire and Water

The following week is a whirlwind, as Karen promised, culminating in a three-day extravaganza called the Triduum—the Church's high holy days.

On Holy Thursday, we remember Jesus' Last Supper and wash each other's feet as he washed the feet of his disciples. This is a sign of humility and servitude—and of stupendous organizational skill, as our church must arrange for a thousand pairs of feet to be washed in less than thirty minutes. Jesus, I believe, would be impressed. The sincerity and speed of this ritual captures the commitment, as well as the success of the Church in serving the poor and sick in our world.

On Good Friday, we are brought to tears as we recall Jesus' painful passion and crucifixion. This is the only day of the year that Mass is not celebrated in the Church, as we mourn Jesus' death. The service features the passing of a large, plain, wooden cross over the heads of the entire congregation. Without intention, I find myself reaching to touch the wood as it goes by.

Then comes the Easter Vigil.

The Church is completely dark. Those who will be baptized are in the front pew in their gray tunics. Their sponsors are directly behind them, each with a hand on the elect's shoulder. I can't see them, but I know they are there because the four candidates for confirmation, myself among them, are seated in the next row, with our sponsors behind, their hands on our shoulders. To our left is a broad tub, brought in especially for the occasion. It is filled with water, and soon will be the center of attention.

From out of the darkness, a single bowl of fire is lit. The

Paschal (or Easter) Candle is lit from the new fire.[6] This thick, six-foot candle, will be lit for every Mass from now until Pentecost, the end of the Season of Easter. Its flame is passed to the parishioners, each of whom holds a small candle in a drip-catcher (to protect the carpet!), and soon the entire church has a flickering glow. We hear a set of Old Testament readings. It is a history of our salvation, beginning with Genesis and the creation of the world. Then we hear the epistle, sing the *Gloria*, peel the bells, and bathe the church in light. The gospel is proclaimed in reverence and majesty. We sing a litany of the saints, and I listen carefully to hear the name of "my" saint, Thérèse of Lisieux.

I can't believe I am here!

Then comes the moment of truth. Father Dan blesses the water in the tub and asks those who are about to be baptized to come forward. He leads them, and us, in the baptismal promises, our profession of faith. Then, one by one, each of the baptismal candidates climbs onto a small footstool and steps into the tub. Clearly, they are both thrilled and embarrassed to be in this position. They glance quickly about the church, kneel into the water, and bend their heads. Father Dan dips a pitcher into the tub and pours the water over their heads three times: in the name of the Father, and of the Son, and of the Holy Spirit. He raises them up from the pool to be dried, like babies, in a large towel. Their hair is a mess, their clothes are sopping wet, and, lo and behold, they are laughing!

Swimming Downstream

Norman Maclean was an author and a fly fisherman who was haunted by water. He closed his famous novella with a beautiful message: "Eventually, all things merge into one, and a river runs through it."[7] "It" meant life, back through all of creation. As I watched the baptism of my peers, with the water sloshing over the tub and running down their tunics, I finally found my image of God. It is a river that flows from God and toward God. It runs, quite literally, through all of us who are a part of God's creation. The water is life-giving, and the river is replenished by love. Perhaps this is circular reasoning, but I have come to understand that God and reason are not always compatible.

I imagine us as fish in this river, and our direction is downstream, toward God. When we let it, the water carries us forward. We can, of course, resist, dipping into eddies or swimming upstream of our own volition. I have come to believe, however, that the natural course is with and toward God, just as our natural state is full immersion in the Source and Summit of all things.

As I watch my wet friends being signed with the oil of chrism, clothed in a white baptismal garment, and given a lit candle to symbolize the Light of Christ, it is the haunting, holy water that I see.

Now Father Dan splashes the whole congregation with holy water, so that we are all a bit damp, which is quite appropriate. At its essence, according to Genesis, the world is made of water. As a people, we were freed and protected by the waters of the Red Sea. Jesus, himself, performed his first public miracle with water. He pulled his first disciples from the water. And he said, quite emphatically, that "no one can enter the kingdom of God without being born of water and the Spirit" (John 3:5). We are, literally, swimming in the stuff.

Down in the Flood

Now Father Dan invites all the candidates for confirmation to come forward with their sponsors. I am surprised to see so many other candidates, for in addition to our RCIA group there are at least twenty others. These folks were raised in the Catholic faith but, for one reason or other, had never been confirmed in it. We stand before the congregation. I feel Doug's hand on my shoulder and I forget, for a moment, that we are not brothers. As I face the congregation for the first time, I see Meri, who is buoyant, and our kids, who seem pretty impressed that Dad gets to stand beside the priest. I repress the urge to sing the *Rocky* theme song. Instead, I simply radiate.

Father Dan lays hands on each of our heads. I feel lightheaded with the touch. The sense of grace takes my breath away, and I remind myself that this is not a good time to faint. Soon, the oil of chrism is applied in two strokes, down and across, on my forehead, and the words of confirmation seem to come up from the waters in the "basement of time"[8]: "Be sealed with the gift of the Holy Spirit." Suddenly, I am confirmed. The gift of conversion has affected us all. Rippling out through Meri to our children, and on to extended families and friends, and even the strangers who put those lovely letters in the vestibule.

Taste and See

We returned to our pews and Doug gives me a bear hug. "The best is yet to come," he says.

I remember Doug describing the moment of first Eucharist as one of the most profound of his life. Other have told me theirs was a celebration for their souls. Indeed, when the church choir starts singing, and the church band cuts in behind, and the full congregation rises from their pews to receive the Eucharist, it feels like a grand parade. We march with the music into the aisles and hold out our hands as we have been taught, right cupped under left. Father Dan raises the Eucharist. "The body of Christ." This time, I know how to respond. "Amen." With the host on my tongue, I go to the chalice. "The blood of Christ." "Amen." I return to the pew, amazed at what has just transpired. I pray.

In the spirit of full confession, though, I must say that I felt no searing revelation at the moment of Eucharist. Maybe the long conversion process was revelation enough. For me, the great awakening occurred in the church parking lot when the water burst from a cracked vase in my mind and covered my doubts in a flood of faith. The Eucharist, itself, is more like a seal—a covenant to not lose what I have finally found.

After Mass, we all embrace. This is indeed a welcome and welcoming family.

CHAPTER 16

Amen to Mystagogy

AMEN!

The RCIA and the Creed end with a word. Each word is distinct, with a different meaning and history, but they carry the same message.

In the Creed, the word is "Amen." It is one of the few words in the Bible that is left virtually untranslated from the original Hebrew. Jesus uses the word liberally to proclaim agreement, or for an emphatic "Yes!" We say "Amen" as well, throughout the Mass, and most particularly, I now know, upon receiving Eucharist. The Nicene Creed closes with this single word. It is a kind of implied question and answer, wrapped into one: Agreed? Are we together on this?

After this year of questions and answers, I can finally respond. I can even recite the Creed with some confidence, which proves that miracles do happen. It is as though I finally understood the lines to a confusing song, or recognized a vaguely familiar face seen long ago through the fractured light of some crystal chandelier. The message is one of affirmation. The answer is *AMEN!*

The last word in the RCIA is also about affirmation, but

this one serves as a platform to forever. From Easter until Pentecost, or longer, churches enter into a period called Mystagogy, which means "leading into the mysteries." The intent is to keep us involved and maintain what one church calls "a pilgrimage of lifelong, continuous conversion."

This is not easy. During my year of conversion, everything was new and the struggle for faith intense. Since then, life has been more profound and more mundane that I could have imagined. I am buoyed by a river of faith that keeps me pointed in the right direction, but the bills, chores, and deadlines of life get in the way, and at times the river seems cluttered and clogged.

A professor at Hartford Seminary, Miriam Therese Winter, suggests a way to keep the journey alive and relevant. She speaks of an idealized Third Testament, one that we create on a daily basis, and that continues through us and future generations. The events of our lives—the births and baptisms, the sufferings and healings—become the unwritten words in this holy book. If more of us understood this relationship between the mundane and the sacred, perhaps there would be more words—more dialogue and discussion between the keepers and the seekers of the faith, those on the fence and those of differing faiths who are on the other side of the fence. That, I believe, is the message of Mystagogy: Keep talking. Amen and mystogogy call us to embrace God's message and to act on the words of the prophets who, in the end, are us—inspired by the Holy Spirit.

The words will always be inspired by God, but they come alive in our own blood, sweat, and tears. In other words, the Word is God's but the words are ours.

Amen....

Endnotes

1. *This is Our Room*, copyright 1993, 2000 by Jesse Manibusan. OPC Publications. All rights reserved.
2. *Open My Eyes*, copyright 1998, 1999 by Jesse Manibusan. OCP Publications. All rights reserved.
3. *Heaven*, copyright 1979 by David Byrne. Blue Disk Music Co., Inc. NY, NY.
4. Bob Dylan, *Highway 61 Revisited*, copyright Special Rider Music, New York, NY. Used with permission.
5. For examples see Dt 12:30-31; 18:9-14; Ps 106:35-39; Jer 19:4-6.
6. Other church communities celebrate variations of the Vigil services.
7. Norman Maclean, *A River Runs Through It*, University of Chicago Press, 2001.
8. Ibid.